Army Cadet
1 Star Training Handbook
2019/20 Edition

PUBLISHING

Knowle Farm Business Centre, Wadhurst Road,
Frant, Tunbridge Wells, Kent, TN3 9EJ
United Kingdom
www.one8e.co.uk • info@one8e.co.uk

ISBN: 9781916097803

Army Cadet: 1 Star Training Handbook
This volume: 1st edition
© Copyright 2019 one8e publishing

Dave Hazlewood has asserted his right
to be identified as the author of this work
in accordance with the Copyright,
Designs and Patents Act 1988

Produced by one8e publishing
Published by one8e publishing
All rights reserved

No part of this publication may be copied or distributed
without prior written permission

Items for photos on loan from www.cadetdirect.com
Thank you to D Company, Kent ACF for photo opportunities

Edited by Samantha Hazlewood
Photography by Mark Roe
Layout by PSD Innovative

Contents

Book guide

This handbook is an unofficial reference guide for instructors, PIs and cadets. All lessons from every subject are covered, along with all testing requirements and a lesson checklist.

Cadets

Cadets should keep this handbook on them at all times. It is designed to be able to fit into combat trousers or combat jacket pockets. Extra notes can be made within the book as lessons are taught, and can be referred to between parade nights to confirm what has been learnt. An adult instructor should sign the lesson checklist on the last page every time a lesson is given. The testing part of the book must be completed under the supervision of an adult instructor.

Instructors & PIs

Instructors are to use this as a reference guide only. The chapter header page for each subject outlines the number of lessons to be delivered as well as the overall aims. There is also a list of where the up to date source material can be found and previous lessons that may need revision. This handbook does not replace the current manuals, but can be used as a handy reference tool when delivering lessons. Lesson plans should still be used to give structure and timings to lessons.

Due to the ever changing nature of the Army Cadet Force, it is wise to check the original source material listed on a regular basis.

The last chapter contains all testing information for every subject, these can be filled in and kept as evidence to enable cadets to sign off their 1 star training.

Feedback

Although every effort has been made to make this publication as accurate as possible, there may be something we've missed. If you spot anything or have any suggestions, please email us so that we can improve future editions.

info@cadetbooks.com

Thanks for reading!

WARNING: Chapter 6 - Skill at arms

Skill at arms lessons are only to be taught by fully qualified, current and competent skill at arms instructors. The information within this book is to be used for reference and revision only and should not be used for giving lessons.

CHAPTER ONE

Aim

By the end of this chapter, you will understand the following:

- Structure of the ACF
- Cadet progress from basic to master cadet

Instructors reference:

- Cadet training manual V1 - Chapter 3 - Sections 7 & 8
- ac71101 - apc (acf) syllabus

Structure of the ACF

The big picture

Having now passed basic training, you hopefully will have been on some sort of training event away from your detachment and met other cadets from around your local area. As you progress, you will meet more and more cadets and understand how you fit into the bigger world of the Army Cadet Force.

With around 39,000 cadets and 9,000 Cadet Force Adult Volunteers (CFAVs) spread over 1,600 detachments, there needs to be a structure in place to make sure things run smoothly.

Organisation

The Army Cadet Force in the UK is split into 57 groupings, known as Counties, Battalions or Sectors. Each grouping is further split down into sub-units called Areas, Companies, Groups or Squadrons. Each of those have several detachments.

Below is an example of just one of the 57 groupings.

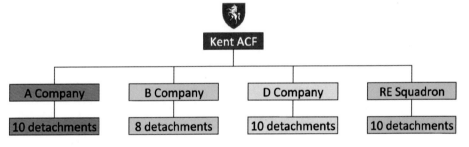

In this example, the over all grouping is Kent (County), which is broken down into four sub-units (three Companies, and one Squadron). Each of these sub units has between eight to ten detachments.

Where do you fit in?

Use the space below to draw a similar plan (called an orbat) of your County/ Battalion/Sector. Also add in where your detachment fits in, and list all other detachments in the same area or company as you.

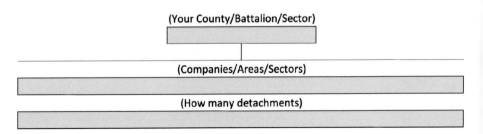

Support

The ACF is run mainly by adult volunteers (CFAVs) who give up their free time to help in different areas of the organisation, but there are also a small number of full time, permanent staff who are paid by the MOD to oversee key areas.

Here are some of the key people at County/Battalion/Sector level:

- **Commandant** - Over all in command of the County/Battalion/Sector.
- **Deputy Commandant** - Second in charge.
- **RSM** - Regimental Sergeant Major - Responsible for discipline and standards.
- **CEO** - Chief Executive Officer - Professional advisor to the Commandant, and responsible for the running of the County/Battalion/Sector HQ.

Here are some of the key people at Company/Area/Sector level:

- **OC** - Officer in Command - Over all in command of the Company/Area/Sector.
- **TO** - Training Officer - Responsible for cadet progress and training events.
- **AO** - Admin Officer - Responsible for accounts and admin.
- **CSM** - Company Sergeant Major - Responsible for discipline and standards.

There are also other organisations that support the ACF:

- **ACFA** - Army Cadet Force Association - A registered charity dedicated to promoting the ideals and activities of the ACF.
- **RFCA** - Reserve Forces & Cadet Association - Looks after a lot of the infrastructure of the ACF and Reserve forces.
- **The British Army** - Provides operational command and funding for the ACF.

Who do you know?

Find out the names of the following staff in your County/Battalion/Sector:

- **Commandant**
- **OC**
- **Deputy Commandant**
- **TO**
- **RSM**
- **AO**
- **CEO**
- **CSM**

Cadet progress

As a basic cadet you would have been given an overview of the APC (Army Proficiency Certificate) syllabus, but here is a bit more detail on what you can expect as you progress through the star levels.

Recruit:

NO BADGE

This is where it all began. As a new recruit, part of your training was probably done without even having full uniform. Everything was brand new, and passing basic training seemed like a real challenge.

Basic passed/one star training:
Having now passed basic training you are now one star training. Most lessons can still be taught and tested at detachment, but some parts will most likely be dealt with on weekends or at annual camp.

One star passed/two star training:
Once you have completed all of the lessons and tests outlined in this book, you will pass one star and start your two star training. Once you have passed one star you are also eligible for promotion to Lance Corporal.

Two star passed/three star training:
A lot of two star training can be done at detachment, but more testing takes place on weekends and camps. You will be expected to set a good example to new cadets and on completion of two star, you will be eligible for promotion to Corporal.

Three star passed/four star training:
Training and testing from this level is mostly done by your County/Battalion/Sector training teams. You will also start to learn Cadet Force Instructional Techniques (CFIT), and pass the Junior Cadet Instructor Cadre (JCIC). After passing three star training, you are eligible for promotion to Sergeant.

Four star passed:
There are no formal lessons to pass four star, but instead you need to specialise in two different subjects and show proof of progressive training. You will also continue CFIT training and the Senior Cadet Instructional Cadre (SCIC). After passing four star the remaining promotion options are also open to you.

Master cadet:
This is the pinnacle for a cadet and not easy to achieve. Only cadets that have proved themselves to be up to the required standard are selected for the one week course at Frimley Park Cadet Training Centre and be in with a chance of achieving this level.

CHAPTER TWO

Aim

By the end of this chapter, you will be competent at the following drill movements:

1. Forming up into 3 ranks & getting on parade

2. Open & close order

3. Wheeling in quick time

4. About turn in quick time

5. Saluting on the march & eyes left/right

6. Dismissing & falling out

Note: When breaking drill sequences down into numbered parts, the squad should call out the number of each movement as they perform it. eg. "SQUAD, ONE", call out "ONE" (Any variation to this is noted within the relevant section).

Instructors reference:

• The Drill manual 2017

• ac71101 - apc (acf) syllabus

Sizing

When forming up as a squad, it is much neater to organise the squad by height. This is called sizing. This can be done at the very start of any parade.

Introductory: **"TALLEST ON THE RIGHT, SHORTEST ON THE LEFT"**

Cautionary: **"IN SINGLE RANK"** Executive: **"SIZE"**

- All cadets line up in one rank with the tallest cadet on the right of the squad (as it faces front), and the shortest on the left. Height is determined by the top of the head dress.

Cautionary: **"FROM THE RIGHT"** Executive: **"NUMBER"**

- Starting with the right marker, each cadet in turn shouts out their number in order.

1 2 3 4 5 6 7 8 9 10 11 12

Right marker

Introductory: **"ODD NUMBERS ONE PACE FORWARD, EVEN NUMBERS ONE PACE BACKWARDS"**

Executive: **"MARCH"**

- All odd numbers (1, 3, 5, 7, 9, 11) take one pace forwards with their left foot.
- All even numbers (2, 4, 6, 8, 10, 12) take one pace backwards with their left foot.

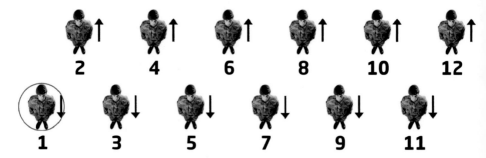

2   4   6   8   10   12

1   3   5   7   9   11

Introductory: **"STAND STILL THE RIGHT MARKER, FRONT RANK TO THE RIGHT, REAR RANK TO THE LEFT"**

Cautionary: **" R A N K S   R I G H T   A N D   L E F T "** Executive: **"TURN"**

- With the exception of the right marker, all odd number cadets turn to their right.

- All even number cadets in the rear rank turn to their left.

Introductory: **"FORM THREE RANKS"**

Cautionary: **" Q U I C K "** Executive: **"MARCH"**

- The front rank marches forward and starts to form three ranks from behind the right marker. The rear rank march around following on from the front rank.

- Cadet 3 becomes the first of the centre rank, and cadet 5 becomes the first of the rear rank. Cadet 7 goes to the front rank and starts the second file, and so on.

- As the front, centre and rear rank of each file gets in place, they all left turn to face front in unison finishing in the position of attention.

Final formation

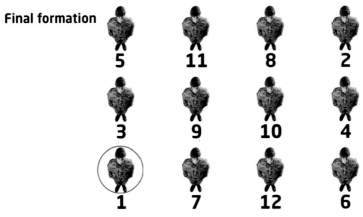

7

Forming up into three ranks

When on parade with enough cadets, you will most likely form up in three ranks. Below is an aerial view of a squad of 12 cadets on parade. The cadet with the circle around them is the 'right marker' (front, right of the squad).

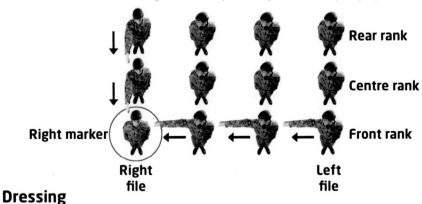

Rear rank

Centre rank

Right marker Front rank

Right file **Left file**

Dressing

When formed up in this manner, cadets must be in neat lines and correctly spaced, which is called dressing. Cadets within the formation line up with those to their right and their front, which is called covering.

Starting in the 'Attention' position, this can be broken down into three stages:

Introductory: **"DRESSING BY NUMBERS"**

Cautionary: **" R I G H T   D R E S S "** Executive: **"ONE"**

- Right file lift their right arm to the front, fists level with their own shoulders.
- Front rank turn their heads to the right and raise their arm to the right, fists level with their own shoulders. Remainder turn their heads to the right.

Cautionary: **" S Q U A D "** Executive: **"TWO"**

- Right file adjust their position until their fist almost touches the person in front.
- Front rank adjust their position until their fist almost touches the person to their right.
- Remainder line up with those in front and to their right.
- Adjustments are made with short, quick steps.

Cautionary: **" E Y E S "** Executive: **"FRONT"**

- Right file and front rank snap their arms back to their sides and everyone faces front at attention, (call out "ONE").

Full words of command:

Introductory: **"DRESSING"** Cautionary: **" R I G H T "** Executive: **"DRESS"**
Followed by: Cautionary: **" E Y E S "** Executive **"FRONT"**

Get on parade

The drill movement 'Get on parade' allows us to put together most of what you have already learnt in one sequence.

Having been sized, start in the 'Stand easy' position in three ranks.

This sequence has no introductory word of command, but has two parts to it.

Cautionary: **" R I G H T "**

- Everyone braces up into the at ease position.

Executive: **"MARKER"**

- The right marker only, comes to attention and marches forward, halting on the 15th pace (same as calling 'Halt' on the 13th pace).

- The right marker then returns to the position of at ease to match the squad.

Imagine hearing the word of command 'HALT' on the 13th step.

1 2 3 4 5 6 7 8 9 10 11 12 13 14 15

Cautionary: **" G E T   O N "** Executive: **"PARADE"**

- The right marker and the rest of the squad come to attention.

- The right marker stays where he is, and the rest of the squad march forward halting on the 15th pace to end up in line (or close) to the right marker.

- The squad then perform the dressing sequence from the previous page with no word of command.

- Once the squad is correctly aligned, the right side of the squad will face front and then return to the position of at ease, followed by the next file, and then the next in turn until the entire squad is facing front and standing at ease.

Open & close order

The spacing between ranks we have been using so far is called 'Close Order'. When inspecting the squad, the ranks with this spacing are too close, so to make more room we can also use 'Open Order'.
This can be learnt in four parts, starting from the position of attention.

Introductory: **"DRESSING BY NUMBERS, IN OPEN ORDER"**

Cautionary: **"R I G H T   D R E S S "** Executive: **"ONE"**

- Leaving their right foot in place, the front rank takes one pace forward with their left foot and the rear rank takes one pace backwards with their left foot.

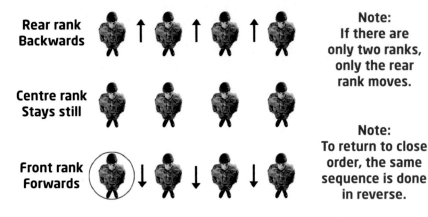

**Rear rank
Backwards**

**Centre rank
Stays still**

**Front rank
Forwards**

**Note:
If there are
only two ranks,
only the rear
rank moves.**

**Note:
To return to close
order, the same
sequence is done
in reverse.**

Cautionary: **" S Q U A D "** Executive: **"TWO"**

- Front and rear ranks lift their right leg and step down into attention.

Cautionary: **" S Q U A D "** Executive: **"THREE"**

- The front rank turn their heads to the right and lift their right arms to the right side, level with their own shoulder.

Cautionary: **" S Q U A D "** Executive: **"FOUR"**

- With the exception of the right file, everyone adjusts their position using short, quick steps to line up with the cadets to their right and front.

Cautionary: **" E Y E S "** Executive: **"FRONT"**

- Front rank snaps their arms back to their sides, and everyone faces front at attention, (call out "ONE").

Full words of command:

Introductory: **"IN OPEN/CLOSE ORDER"** Cautionary: **"RIGHT"** Executive: **"DRESS"**
Followed by: Cautionary: **"EYES"** Executive **"FRONT"**

Wheeling in quick time

As a basic training cadet, you learnt how to march and halt over a short distance. There will however be times when you will march over longer distances such as when on official parades or around a camp, where you may need to change direction. To negotiate bends in roads, or to march around the perimeter of a parade square, you will need to be able to 'wheel' left or right.

Cautionary: **" R I G H T "**

Executive: **"WHEEL"**

- The cautionary and executive words of command are given over one full pace.
- On hearing the word of command 'wheel', the cadet on the front right of the squad will change direction and shorten their pace.
- All other cadets on the right hand side will also shorten their pace and follow on.
- Cadets in the centre will maintain a normal pace, but will follow the change of direction while maintaining formation.
- Cadets on the left hand side will have to widen their pace slightly to follow the change of direction and maintain formation.

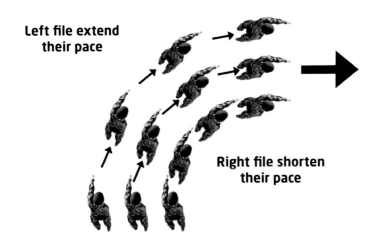

Left file extend their pace

Right file shorten their pace

Points to note::

- To wheel to the left, carry out the exact same process but to the opposite side.
- If you are to wheel less than 90 degrees, the word of command **"FORWARD'** will be given when the front rank are travelling in the correct direction.
- If you are to wheel greater than 90 degrees, the words of command to wheel may be given again, followed by **"FORWARD"** when the front rank are travelling in the correct direction.

About turn in quick time

When a marching squad needs to turn 180 degrees in a smaller area, there may not be enough space to wheel. In this case the squad will need to perform an about turn without coming to a halt.

This sequence can be broken down into parts and learnt by numbers.

Start from a frozen marching position with the right foot forward.

Introductory: **"TURNINGS, BY NUMBERS"**

Cautionary: **"A B O U T   T U R N"** Executive: **"ONE"**

- Take one full pace with the left foot.
- Take half a pace with the right foot and step down into the position of attention, but with the right foot slightly forward (heel of the right foot touching the instep of the left).
- Squad calls out "IN".

Cautionary: **"S Q U A D"** Executive: **"TWO"**

- Lift the left leg, pivot 90 degrees to the right on the heel of the right foot and step down into the position of attention facing the right side.
- Squad calls out "LEFT".

PRACTICE THIS SEQUENCE UNTIL THE SQUAD IS HAPPY WITH IT AND THEN COMBINE BOTH PARTS INTO ONE COUNT. THE FULL SEQUENCE CAN THEN BE PRACTICED AS FOLLOWS:

Introductory: **"TURNINGS, BY NUMBERS"**

Cautionary: **"A B O U T   T U R N"** Executive: **"ONE"**

- Carry out both movements previously practiced.
- Squad calls out "IN" - "LEFT".

Cautionary: **" S Q U A D "** Executive: **"TWO"**

- Lift the right leg, pivot 90 degrees to the right on the heel of the left foot and step down into the position of *attention, now having turned a full 180 degrees.
- Squad calls out "RIGHT".

(*Amended May 2020)

Cautionary: **" S Q U A D "** Executive: **"THREE"**

- Lift the left leg and step down into the position of attention again, ready to march off.
- Squad calls out "LEFT".

Cautionary: **" S Q U A D "** Executive: **"FORWARD"**

- Step off with the right foot and continue marching.
- Squad calls out "FORWARD".

Note:

These words of command are only given when learning the sequence by numbers, but when practicing at full speed, it is still good practice to get the squad to call out "IN, LEFT, RIGHT, LEFT, FORWARD" as they perform the sequence to improve timings with the squad.

When performing this sequence on the march without breaking it down, the word of command "TURN" is given as heel of the right foot hits the ground.

Full words of command:

Introductory: **"TURNINGS"** Cautionary: **" A B O U T "** Executive: **"TURN"**

Saluting on the march

As a basic cadet you learnt how to salute to the front while standing at attention, now we look at saluting on the march.

Saluting by numbers

Before attempting the full sequence, it is possible to first learn it by numbers.

Start at a frozen marching position with the left foot forward.

Introductory: **"SALUTING BY NUMBERS"**

Cautionary: **"S A L U T E   T O   T H E   R I G H T"** Executive: **"ONE"**

- Take one pace forward with the right foot and swing your arms as normal.

- Then take one pace forward with the left foot, at the same time turn your head to the right and bring the right hand up to salute making sure both eyes can see the palm of your hand. Left arm snaps to your side. Freeze in this position.

Cautionary: **"S Q U A D"** Executive: **"TWO"**

- Maintain this upper body position and step forward with your right foot.

Cautionary: **"S Q U A D"** Executive: **"THREE"**

- Maintain this upper body position and step forward with your left foot.

Cautionary: **"S Q U A D"** Executive: **"FOUR"**

- Maintain this upper body position and step forward with your right foot.

Cautionary: **"S Q U A D"** Executive: **"FIVE"**

- Maintain this upper body position and step forward with your left foot.

Cautionary: **"S Q U A D"** Executive: **"SIX"**

- Step forward with your right foot, turn your head to the front and bring your right arm down so both arms are as they would be when at attention, (call out "DOWN").

Cautionary: **"S Q U A D"** Executive: **"FORWARD"**

- Step forward with your left foot and swing your right arm to the front and your left arm to the rear. This is where you would continue marching, (call out "SWING").

Saluting to the left

When saluting to the left, follow the exact same sequence but to the left.

Full words of command:

Introductory: **"SALUTING"** Cautionary: **"S A L U T E   T O   T H E   R I G H T/ L E F T"** Executive: **"SALUTE"**

Saluting on the march - Full sequence

- The word of command **"SALUTE"** is given as the left heel strikes the ground.

- There are no further words of command after this, but when practicing, it is good to get the squad to call out timings: **1 - 2 - 3 - 4 - 5 - DOWN - SWING.**

Saluting an officer on the march

When a squad of cadets are marching, and an officer is spotted, the words of command "SALUTE" - "UP" are given by the cadet nearest the officer. The word "UP" is given as the left heel hits the floor. The cadets then march another five paces and then follow the same procedure for saluting on the march.

Saluting to the front

It is sometimes required for an individual cadet to approach an officer to deliver a message or receive an award etc. This can be practiced while marching as a squad.

Introductory: **"SALUTING"**

Cautionary: **" S A L U T E   T O   T H E   F R O N T "** Executive: **"SALUTE"**

- In this instance the word of command "SALUTE" is given as the right foot passes the left, and is exactly the same as when hearing the word of command "HALT".

- Halt as normal, then salute twice (with the correct timings for saluting at the halt).

- About turn and march off.

NOTE: When saluting an officer or standard, it is normal to turn to the right and march off instead of doing an about turn, so as not to turn your back on them.

Eyes right (or left)

Sometimes when a compliment is needed while marching, only the NCO or officer in charge of the squad will be the person to salute, with everyone else just turning their heads in the required direction.

The sequence for this is exactly the same as for saluting on the march except the head turns with no salute, and both arms go to the position of attention.

Introductory: **"BY THE RIGHT"** (OR LEFT)

Cautionary: **" E Y E S "** Executive: **"RIGHT"** (OR LEFT)

NOTE:
In some instances, more than 5 paces may be required when paying a compliment on the march, in this case the compliment is held until the words of command 'EYES FRONT" are called. This will be called as the left foot strikes the ground. Swing arms and return to marching the next time the left heel strikes the ground.

If a cadet has injured their right hand, they are allowed to salute with the left hand.

When not wearing headdress, do not salute with the hand, but instead brace up into the position of attention. If walking, perform eyes right/left for 5 paces.

Dismissing & falling out

At the end of a parade, cadets will be given the words of command 'Dismiss' or 'Fall out', depending on what is happening after that parade.

Fall out - Leave the parade but you will be returning at some point (eg. at the end of the first parade at detachment).

Dismiss - Leave the parade and you will not be required again (eg. at the end of the final parade at detachment).

The sequence for both commands is the same and can be broken into 3 parts.

Introductory: **"DISMISSING/FALLING OUT BY NUMBERS"**

Cautionary: **" D I S M I S S / F A L L O U T "** Executive: **"ONE"**

- Everyone turns to the right leaving their feet in the same position as if performing a right turn by numbers.

Cautionary: **" S Q U A D "** Executive: **"TWO"**

- Everyone lifts their left leg and then steps down into the position of attention facing the right.

Cautionary: **" S Q U A D "** Executive: **"FORWARD"**

- Everyone marches forward 3 full paces calling out "LEFT, RIGHT, LEFT" as they go.

- After the 3 paces, everyone breaks away.

NOTE:

- When falling out, no-one is to leave the area of the parade square/detachment.

- When being dismissed, everyone is then free to leave.

- If there is an officer present when being dismissed (not when falling out), everyone is to salute to the front before taking the 3 paces.

Full words of command:

Executive: **"FALL OUT" or "DISMISS"**

CHAPTER THREE

Aim

By the end of this chapter, you will have received the following lessons:

1.a. Maintaining clothing & equipment

1.b. Personal hygiene

1.c. Feeding in the field

2. Shelter

3. Why things are seen

4. Cam & concealment

5. Observation

6. Judging distance

7. Range cards

8. Indication of targets

9. Duties of a sentry

10. Moving with/without weapons

11. Field signals

12. Elementary obstacle crossing

13. Selecting a route across country

14. Introduction to night training

15. Elementary night movement

16. Stalking

17. Reaction to fire control orders

Instructors reference:

- Fieldcraft & Tactics 71966
- Fieldcraft & Tactics (syllabus) 71101
- Skill at arms pamphlet 71807-C

Administration in the field

Maintaining weapons, clothing and equipment

Fieldcraft is all about team work, but each individual cadet must be able to look after themselves, their clothing and their equipment. If they cannot do this, they will experience issues that will impact on them and the rest of the team.

Personal weapon

This must be kept with you at ALL times, and should be maintained in line with the skill at arms syllabus.

Clothing

- All clothing worn or packed must be clean and in good condition.
- Only pack essential spare clothing and make sure that it is all kept in waterproof bags. (Use simple plastic bags or specific 'dry bags'). Keep these stored in your CEMO unless needed, as they may reflect light and be easy to see.
- Change socks and underwear daily.
- Pack waterproofs and use them when needed to keep your main clothes dry.
- If your clothing gets wet, change into dry clothing and keep the wet clothing separate. It may be possible to dry damp clothing using body heat by leaving it in the bottom of your sleeping bag overnight.

Equipment

- Check zip on sleeping bag, make sure it has been aired and keep it waterproof.
- Check straps, clips, buckles etc. on all carrying equipment.
- Spare straps, bungees, paracord and sniper (cloth) tape can be useful for repairs.

Dry bags   **Paracord**   **Bungees**   **Sniper (cloth) tape**

Good preparation and maintenance of kit can make the difference between a great fieldcraft experience and a miserable one.

Maintaining standards of personal hygiene

As well as clothing and equipment, cadets need to look after themselves.

Personal cleanliness

- **Hair:** Should ideally be kept short to allow treatment of any head injuries, and to prevent parasites. It should be washed at least once per week.
- **Face:** Washed daily. (Boys also need to shave daily).
- **Teeth:** Need to be cleaned twice per day, and if possible after meals.
- **Body:** Needs to be washed daily. Ensure areas where sweat can build up such as armpits and groin are cleaned to avoid rashes or fungal infections. Use showers when on camp, but use a flannel when out in the field.
- **Feet:** Keep clean, dry and powdered to avoid blisters or infections. Keep toe nails short to avoid in-growing toe nails. Change socks daily.
- **Cuts and injuries:** Make sure these are kept clean and fresh plasters or dressings are applied regularly.
- **Sanitation:** Only use the toilets provided on the training area, and make sure to clean hands thoroughly after use.

Food preparation

Preparing food outside requires the highest standards of hygiene. If this doesn't happen, there is a greater risk of becoming ill.

- Clean hands before handling any food.
- Only use food from ration packs. Don't supplement with anything else.
- Clean mess tins and eating utensils after every use.
- Throw all rubbish away in designated areas, or keep your own rubbish bag.
- Don't leave any food stuff out as it may attract insects and rodents.
- Always keep your cooking area clear and tidy.

Water

- Only drink issued (safe) water.
- Puritabs in ration packs are for emergency use only.
- If there is an emergency, water can also be boiled for 10 minutes to make it safe. Any scum formed on the top must also be removed.

Feeding in the field

When on fieldcraft exercises you will be issued genuine British Army 24 hour Multi Climate ration packs (MCR). Each box contains enough food to sustain a regular soldier in the field for 24 hours and has all the nutritional requirements required. A cadet may not need to consume everything from a box, but the main meals and snacks need to be eaten to maintain energy levels and stay healthy. There's a lot of variety so there's something for everyone.

NOTE: Make sure to inform your instructors if you have any dietary requirements. There are vegetarian, kosher and halal versions available.

Breakfast
Boil in the bag meal, pastry or an 'add cold water' cereal.

Lunch
Boil in the bag light meal or a savoury snack.

Main meal
Boil in the bag meal and a desert.

Snacks
Savoury and sweet snacks.

Drinks
Hot and cold powdered drinks with sugar and creamer.

Extras
Hand wipes, tissues, dental gum, matches etc.

When you first open your ration box, it is a good idea to separate out what you are having for each meal, and put some snacks where they are easy to get to. Only ever have out what you need and make sure you get rid of all rubbish.

All meals are designed to be eaten hot or cold, so no harm will come to you if you don't heat your meals thoroughly. It's always much nicer to have a nice hot meal after a tough days training though.

When you are issued with your rations you will also be issued an operational ration heater stove along with operational ration heater fuel. These are potentially very dangerous if used incorrectly so the utmost care must be taken.

IMPORTANT: The following information is a guide only. Cadets are to be given clear instructions and demonstrations from qualified CFAVs on how to use the stove and fuel, and are to be observed at all times when first attempting to prepare meals.

Stove
Folds out for cooking
and has a built in
windshield. Can
store fuel in when
not in use.

Fuel
DO NOT EAT
Clean fuel that burns
extremely hot. Light
with care.

Cooking process

- Prepare the ground: Clear a safe area twice the size of the stove to cook on. Remove twigs and anything that may be flammable. Dig a small hole if needed, but replace soil afterwards.

- Unfold the stove and place in an open area (not under a basha or enclosed space). Make sure it is stable.

- Remove one fuel gel carefully and place into the centre part of the stove. Light from an arms length away using the wind-proof matches included in the ration pack, or a lighter or flint. One gel will last for around 5 - 8 minutes which is long enough to boil water for a meal and/or drink.

- Place meal pouch (unopened and not damaged) to be heated into a mess tin and cover with water. Do not overfill as it may boil over and cause injury.

- Carefully place the mess tin onto the stove to heat. Another mess tin can also be used to cover the main tin and speed up cooking time, but take care when removing.

- After approximately five minutes, carefully remove the pouch using the 'spork' provided in the ration pack or a multi-tool. The pouch will be hot so a glove or cloth can be used to hold the pouch while opening it. Use the remaining hot water to make a hot drink or for washing with. Use the spork to eat the meal.

- After cooking, make sure to clean all utensils properly before packing away, and clear away any rubbish. Make sure the ground doesn't show any signs of you having been there at all. The plastic bag that held some of your ration contents is good for keeping rubbish in until you get back to camp.

- Never miss meals and make sure to keep taking on fluids. Hot drinks in cold weather help warm you up from the inside, and cold drinks in hot weather keeps you hydrated.

Tactical cooking

When on an exercise that is tactical (potential enemy threat), you need to take extra care. Make sure sentries are in place, cooking is done in daylight where possible, and you do not burn anything that could make a strong smell or create smoke. Digging a small hole for the stove can also reduce light given from flames. In extreme cases a 'hard routine' can be followed which means eating meals cold.

Shelter

Shelter when sleeping out in the field is basic but doesn't need to be uncomfortable. A well constructed 'basha' can provide adequate shelter from the elements and help maintain morale when you start to feel tired or cold.

This is what you will need, ideally packed away into one small bag or stuff sack:

Basha or Poncho	**Bungees or paracord**	**Tent pegs**	**Basha poles**
X 1	**X 4 - 6**	**X 6 - 8**	**X 2**
Rectangular sheet of camouflage, waterproof material.	Used to hold the basha or poncho in place.	Used to fix the bottom of the basha or poncho to the ground.	Not always needed but handy when there are no trees.

Construction

There are several ways to construct your shelter, but here are the two most common. Make sure the opening faces out so that you can observe and defend if needed. Your shelter should be packed away during daylight hours or camouflaged to conceal it.

'Lean-to'

This design opens on one side and is fixed to the ground on the other. It only provides partial protection from the elements, but is easy to get in and out of, and provides good visibility and arcs of fire if needed.

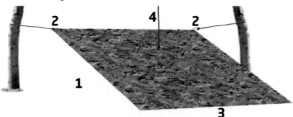

1. Clear the ground of any sharp stones, twigs or branches that may damage your equipment, or cause discomfort when sleeping.

2. Attach two corners of one end of the basha or poncho to two trees about knee height.

3. Fix the opposite side to the ground using tent pegs.

4. To avoid water collecting on the sheet if it rains, lift the middle of the sheet by attaching bungees or paracord to the middle of the sheet and connect to an overhead branch.

'A-Frame'

This design is open at either end, which provides much better protection from the elements, but is not as easy to get in and out of and doesn't have as good visibility.

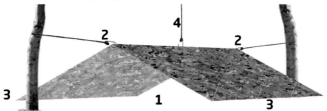

1. Clear the ground of any sharp stones, twigs or branches that may damage your equipment, or cause discomfort when sleeping.

2. Attach two corners of the middle of the basha or poncho to two trees about knee height.

3. Fix both opposite sides to the ground using tent pegs.

4. To avoid water collecting on the sheet if it rains, lift the middle of the sheet by attaching bungees or paracord to the middle of the sheet and connect to an overhead branch.

Sleeping

Once your shelter is built, you have a covered place to sleep and leave your extra kit. Here are the other items you will now need:

Sleeping bag	**Sleeping mat**	**Bivvy bag**
Needs to be a high quality, three/four season sleeping bag, designed for outdoor use.	Small and portable, this will insulate you from the ground. Without it, the ground is very cold.	This is a waterproof cover for your sleeping bag. It improves insulation and water resistance.

The harbour area

The area used to perform personal admin such as cleaning, eating and sleeping, is a tactical 'harbour' area. This is an area that may need to be defended if attacked, but is set up and organised to minimise that chance. To aid this, you need to work tidy, only have out what you need at that moment and clear up after yourself.

When leaving the harbour, leave it as if no-one had ever been there. Clear rubbish, cover tracks and cooking areas and don't leave anything behind.

Why things are seen

Things are easy or difficult to see based on several factors.

1. Shape

Some things have such obvious shapes, they can easily be seen. **Examples:**

- Outline of a person.

- Clear shape of items such as weapons and helmets.

- Hard lines of shelters.

Use camouflage to disguise obvious shapes

2. Silhouette

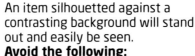
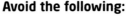

An item silhouetted against a contrasting background will stand out and easily be seen. **Avoid the following:**

- Smooth flat backgrounds such as water, plain fields or sky.

- Backgrounds with contrasting colour.

Use uneven backgrounds with natural colours to match your camouflage

3. Texture

Items with a contrasting texture to its surrounding stands out. **Examples:**

- Shiny objects such as mess tins and skin (even dark skin).

- Reflective surfaces.

Use camouflage to help conceal shiny or reflective surfaces

4. Shadow

Sunlight casts shadows, which can be good or bad depending on how they are used.

- **Good:** Stay in shadows to remain unseen.
- **Bad:** Don't let your shadow protrude from cover and give away your position.

Use shadows to your advantage

5. Spacing

Items in nature are very rarely evenly spaced. **Even spacing is obvious in the following:**

- When patrolling.
- When forming defensive positions.

Vary your distance from each other to avoid even spacing

6. Movement

Movement can attract the eye and allow you to be seen when you are otherwise concealed. **Examples:**

- Moving between cover.
- Disturbing trees/vegetation when moving.

Avoid sudden, fast movements, and be careful of disturbing vegetation around you

Personal camouflage and concealment

Now that we understand why things are seen, we can use camouflage and concealment to make ourselves harder to see when operating out in the field. This will enable us to observe without being observed.

Camouflage - Disguising our appearance to help blend in with our surroundings.

Concealment - Using our environment to hide our location.

Personal Camouflage

1. Evenly apply brown camouflage cream to any exposed skin (hands, face neck) to remove shine.

(Texture)

2. Apply random lines of darker brown and green to disguise the recognisable shape of your features.

(Shape)

3. Use foliage from your immediate surroundings to disguise the shape of your body and equipment.

(Shape)

Note the following:

• Make sure when applying camouflage (cam) cream, you apply enough to do the job, without adding too much as this can actually make you easier to see.

• Apply more cam cream at night than during the day as skin can be more visible in dim light.

• Use string, elastic or natural loops in clothing and equipment to affix foliage, but don't add too much as this may restrict movement and may make you stand out. Make sure the foliage matches your background and change it when needed.

• Weapons are already camouflaged so shouldn't need anything extra, however, if you decide to add anything to disguise its shape, be careful not to do anything that will be difficult to remove, or may impair how it works.

Concealment

1. Look through cover and not around or over it, as this will break the line of cover and show your position.

2. Avoid using isolated cover as it is easy for an enemy to identify and direct fire onto your position. Choose positions that are harder to identify.

3. Imagine viewing your position from an enemy point of view. What is behind you? Do you blend in? Avoid backgrounds that make you stand out.

Observation

Observation is a key skill that cadets must acquire when operating out in the field. It is the ability to systematically scan an area to search for enemy positions or potential threats. It is not difficult, it just needs the correct approach to be effective.

Scanning

Below is a photo of a landscape similar to a location within a training area. When observing an area such as this, follow these simple steps:

- Divide the view into 'Near', Middle' and 'Far'.

- Search the near ground first as this has the greatest threat.

- Start scanning slowly with your eyes, from bottom left to bottom right, then scan back from right to left a little higher, slightly overlapping the area just scanned.

- Continue scanning left to right, a little higher, and then back a little higher again.

- Do this until all of the near ground has been scanned, then move onto the middle ground, and then the far ground.

Far — Search here last.

Middle — Search here second.

Near — Search here first.

Start bottom left. Scan with your eyes along, up, along, up etc. until you have scanned the whole scene. Make sure to overlap your scan to avoid missing areas.

When scanning, identify areas that may have a potential threat, or that look unusual. Remember why things are seen, and look further into anything that stands out.

Judging distance

When observing an area, or when under attack from an enemy, it may be necessary for you to let others know what you have seen. To do this you need to be able to give an estimated distance away from where you are situated.

Judging distance by unit of measure

The most common form of measurement for this is the metric system which uses centimetres, metres and kilometres.

- 1 centimetre (cm) is made up of 10 millimetres (mm).
- 1 metre is made up of 100 centimetres (cm), or 1000 millimetres (mm).
- 1 kilometre is made up of 1000 metres.

When judging how far away something is, it is useful to remember how large certain common items are so that you can imagine how many of those items would fit into the distance you are trying to estimate.

Here are a few approximate sizes of some common items to get you started:

Car	**Bus/coach**	**Aeroplane**	**Football pitch**
5 metres	15 metres	50 metres	100 metres

When judging a distance, imagine these objects between you and the point you are looking at. For example, if you think you could fit two coaches between you and that location then a guess of approximately 30 metres is pretty good. If you think you could fit three football pitches between you and the location, then 300 metres is probably about right.

Judging distance by appearance

Understanding how things appear as they get further away can also help you estimate distance. Here is a guide to how a person looks at different intervals.

- 100m: Clear.
- 200m: Fairly clear with skin colour and equipment easily identifiable.
- 300m: Clear body outline and skin colour, but other details blurred.
- 400m: Body outline clear, but everything else is blurred.
- 500m: Body begins to taper and the head becomes indistinct.
- 600m: Body now looks wedge shaped and head cannot be identified.

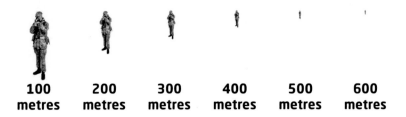

| 100 metres | 200 metres | 300 metres | 400 metres | 500 metres | 600 metres |

Conditions affecting appearance

Objects seem closer: The following can make objects seem closer:

- The sun is shining bright behind you.
- The object you are looking at is much bigger than other things near them.
- There is dead ground (open space) between you and the object being observed.
- The object being observed is higher up than you.

Objects seem further away: The following can make objects seem further away:

- There is bad light, or the sun is in your eyes.
- The object you are looking at is smaller than other things around them.
- You are looking across a valley or down a street.
- You are lying down.

Aids to judging distance

Here are a few other tips to help when judging distances:

- Key ranges: Knowing how far away certain key locations are in your view, can help you estimate more accurately. Using a map for example will allow you to work out using grid squares how far away something is, and then relate that to other things around.

- Bracketing: If you are really unsure of a distance, estimate the maximum distance it could possibly be and then the minimum distance. Take the mid point of the two to get your estimate. E.g. maximum distance of 300 metres and a minimum distance of 100 metres, would make your estimate 200 metres (between 100 and 300).

- Halving: When estimating longer distances, try working out the distance to the half way point of where you are, and then doubling that to get your full estimate.

- Group average: When in a group, it is a good idea to get everyone to make an estimate, and then take an average of everyones ideas to get a final estimate.

Range cards

If observing an area for a long period of time, you may want to draw up a small sketch of what you see and add a few notes and distances to help yourself and others get familiar with the ground. This is useful in several instances, such as when carrying out the role of a sentry, when in an observation post, or when doing any sort of reconnaissance (observing enemy positions).

Here is the scene from the observation section with a few simple names given to obvious locations in the near and middle ground.

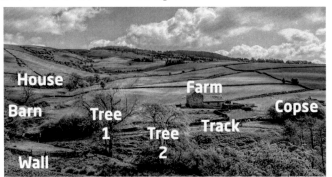

The template for your sketch map is called a range card and has curved lines that represent increments in distance. Below is a simple range card made to represent the scene above with each curved line representing 10 metres. The middle point at the bottom would be your observation point.

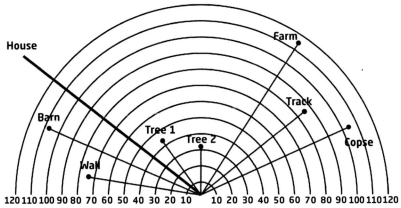

- The straight lines represent the angles from you to the various locations.

- Each curved line on this card represents 10 metres, but they could represent 100 metres if you were doing a range card on a larger scale.

- The thick line to the house is a 'setting ray' and helps orientate your range card.

- For more detail, a full circle range card can be used to plot a full 360 degree view.

Indication of targets

It's good to understand how to observe an area and judge distances, but there may be instances where you see something no-one else does and you need to indicate a location to others. This may be when under attack and you are the only person that has seen the enemy.

To indicate a target to others, you must be clear, loud and precise. There are several ways to do this, but the order of delivery is always the same.

1. Range (distance away) in metres: e.g. "100"

2. Indication (direction/where to look). e.g. " Left of Farm"

The method of giving the location depends on how well you know the ground and how easy the target location is to explain. If you are attacked in a location you have been observing for a while, and have identified some key locations, indicating a target will be far easier than when on a patrol and being attacked in an unknown area.

Reference points

The key features identified while observing (farm, copse etc.), are the easiest ways to identify a target. A target located near one of those would be easy to indicate.

Arc of fire

Arcs break your view into areas that are quick and easy for everyone to identify. You won't visually see these arcs, but instead need to imagine them in front of you.

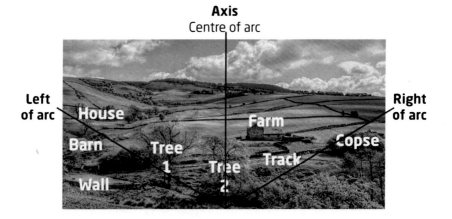

In the example above, there are lots of details to refer to when identifying a target. You can give a range (distance) of the target and then identify their location using a reference point or an arc. Either options would work just as well.
e.g. **"100" - "Copse" - "Enemy"** or **"100" - "Right of Arc" "Enemy"**

Direct method

This method of identifying targets is called the 'direct method', and is good when the target location is fairly obvious. When the target location is less obvious, or is in an unknown area, you can further break down your arc to help describe other areas in your view.

Below is a more detailed breakdown of an arc of fire. Using the example from the previous page, if you applied this detailed arc, you could identify targets in the open areas and spaces between key features a lot easier.

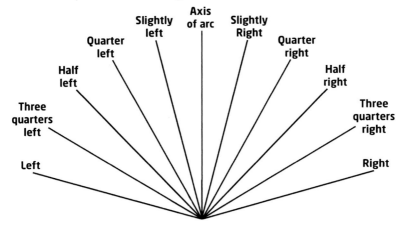

Clock ray method

Another method of identifying targets is to imagine a clock face over one of your reference points, and give a direction from that.

In the example above, imagine a target 90 metres away by a low wall, down and right of the farmhouse. The indication could be as follows:

"90" - "Farm - 5 o'clock - small wall" - "Enemy"

Examples

Using all of the previous methods, here are a few examples of target indication.

House
Farm
Barn
Tree 1
Copse
Track
Tree 2
Wall

Remember: RANGE then INDICATION

1. Reference method:
   "120" - "House" - "Enemy"

2. Reference method:
   "90" - "Front of barn" - "Enemy"

3. Direct method
   "400" - "Centre of arc - Left of woods" - "Enemy"

4. Direct method -
   "300" - "Quarter right - Corner of wall" - "Enemy"

5. Clock ray method
   "200" - "Copse - 11 o'clock - Small trees" - "Enemy"

Other methods

The methods for identifying targets looked at so far will probably be all you need as a cadet, but there are other methods should you wish to develop this further.

- **Hand angles:** Holding your arm out in front of you, you can work out how many degrees difference there is between two locations by seeing how many fingers or knuckles fit between them.

- **Binoculars:** Good quality binoculars show degrees which can help in the same way as hand angles.

Duties of a sentry

When in a harbour area, certain cadets will be tasked with providing security while the others attend to personal admin, eat meals or catch up on sleep. This is known as 'sentry duty', and all cadets will take turns at some point in being a sentry.

Around the outside of a harbour area, there may be up to three sentry positions, each manned by two cadets. All will watch their front arcs for any enemy movement and check returning patrols are friendly (not an enemy patrol). The sentry post needs to be camouflaged, but must have a good field of vision. A range card is normally drawn up to show key features in front of the position and help to identify targets as described in the previous chapter.

Staggered duty

Cadets take it in turns to be sentries for periods of around one hour each. This happens all day and night and at times can be extremely tiring, but being alert and observant is essential. To help with this the section 2IC (2nd in command) draws up a 'Stag list' of names with timings, but arranges it so that changeovers are staggered (both cadets don't change at the same time). This means that as one cadet hands over to a new sentry, the other maintains observation. It also means that one cadet is always fresher and more awake than the other.

Time	Names	
2200	Cadet 1	
2230		Cadet 2
2300	Cadet 3	
2330		Cadet 4
0000	Cadet 5	
0030		Cadet 6
0100	Cadet 7	
0130		Cadet 8
0200		

Here is a section from a Stag list for one sentry post. As you can see, cadet 1 starts their duty at 2200 and finishes at 2300, with cadet 2 starting their duty half way through at 2230. This then continues with half the cadets starting their duties on the hour, and the other half starting at half past the hour.

On an actual stag list, real cadets names would be in place of 'Cadet 1', 'Cadet 2' etc. and the list would cover a much longer period of time.

Equipment needed

- Stag list
- Binoculars (if available)
- Range card
- Whistle
- Torch
- Map & compass
- Communications - radios, or a 'Comms cord' which is a length of paracord connected back to the IC.

35

Information needed

In order for a sentry to be effective, they need to know certain information as without it, security could be compromised. Some of this will be on the range card.

- Where and when they need to be on duty.
- Procedure for changeover.
- Location of section commander and how to contact them.
- Names of key features in front of them (range card).
- Arcs of observation and fire.

- Procedure for challenging approaching patrols or troops.
- Direction of any known enemy threat.
- Details of any known friendly patrols.
- Positions of other sentry posts.
- Current password and time it changes (see below).

Password

To help identify friendly patrols and troops attempting to enter the harbour area, a password is set every 24 hours at 1200. The password is normally a four letter word spelt out in two halves using the phonetic alphabet.

Example: **STAR** = **S**ierra - **T**ango - **A**lpha - **R**omeo

- **Challenge:** Sentry states **"Sierra, Tango"**
- **Reply:** Approaching troops or patrol leader states **"Alpha, Romeo"**

Phonetic alphabet

This is a system used when spelling out words to ensure accuracy. Every letter of the alphabet has a word associated with it that starts with that corresponding letter.

To help you create and understand passwords, here is the full phonetic alphabet.

A	ALPHA	H	HOTEL	O	OSCAR	V	VICTOR
B	BRAVO	I	INDIA	P	PAPA	W	WHISKEY
C	CHARLIE	J	JULIETT	Q	QUEBEC	X	X-RAY
D	DELTA	K	KILO	R	ROMEO	Y	YANKEE
E	ECHO	L	LIMA	S	SIERRA	Z	ZULU
F	FOXTROT	M	MIKE	T	TANGO		
G	GOLF	N	NOVEMBER	U	UNIFORM		

Points to note:

- The challenge may be given twice in conditions where it may be difficult to hear, but if the sentry is not satisfied with the reply, the orders for opening fire may be followed.
- Visual identification and questioning can also be used to confirm identity.

Challenging

When a sentry sees a patrol or individual approaching the harbour area, they need to confirm they are friendly forces and not an enemy patrol trying to get closer or infiltrate the area. To do this, the sentry must take control of the situation and verify the identity of whoever it is, whatever rank.

This flowchart explains the sequence to follow on seeing a body of troops approach the sentry position. The password is STAR (Sierra - Tango - Alpha - Romeo).

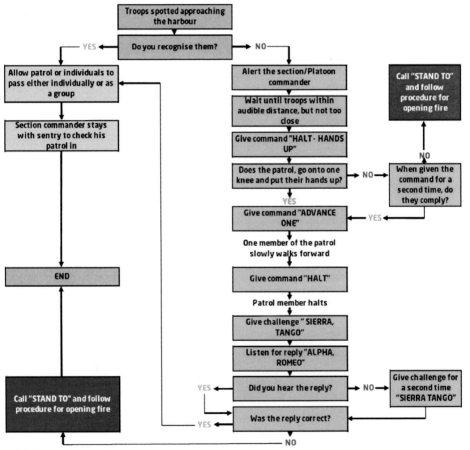

Other scenarios

If a sentry spots an enemy presence that hasn't seen the harbour area or sentry position, the immediate commander is to be told straight away and they will ensure that everyone is quietly stood to in case of an attack.

If there is an obvious attack happening on the harbour, the sentry skips to the last stage of the flowchart and calls "STAND TO" and opens fire.

Moving with or without personal weapons

We previously looked at why things are seen, and how to use camouflage and concealment to blend in to our surroundings. How we move can have a major effect on this too. E.g. fast movement draws the eye and can create more noise, both of which will compromise our ability to remain undetected.

Here are three methods of movement:

1. Tactical walk

This is the most common method of movement, used when an enemy threat is possible but not definite. This is not just a stroll though, and placement of feet, and noise created while moving need to be considered. You need to be alert at all times, with your rifle held securely so it can be used immediately if needed. Keep your head up and look around at your surroundings as you walk, and turn your body as well as your head as you observe.

2. Monkey run

This method of movement allows you to keep a lower profile and move behind low cover without being detected. Your feet, knees and hands (knuckles) are all in contact with the ground. Move one limb at a time, placing your knees where your hands have been. Avoid dragging your feet.

3. Leopard crawl

This method of movement is used when you need to keep low to the ground. Shift your weight from side to side using your opposite knee and elbow to move forward. Make sure not to lift your body as you move forward. With a rifle, you can carry it by holding the pistol grip and hand-guard, or by holding it across both arms.

Points to note:

- For maximum stealth, move slowly and watch the ground for anything that will make a noise if you disturb it. Keep your head up and observe all around you.

- Be careful with your rifle to avoid knocking the safety catch, releasing the magazine, damaging the sights or getting dirt into the muzzle.

- When moving with a weapon, ensure the sling is fitted correctly and hold by the pistol grip or the main point of balance.

Patrolling with a section, the basics

Patrolling is not something that is officially looked at during one star training, but is worth mentioning as it has relevance to several of the sections that you do look at.

The section

A section is a small group of cadets that can operate as a small unit for various tasks and objectives. Made up ideally of around 8 cadets, there are several roles to be fulfilled:

- **Section commander x 1:** This will be a CFAV or senior cadet and is in command (IC) of the section.

- **Section second in command (2IC) x 1:** This will also be a CFAV or senior cadet.

- **Riflemen x 6:** This will be your initial role within the section and you will take direction from the IC or 2IC. Riflemen can also fill other roles such as the scout who is the lead person on a patrol.   Platoon IC = A
Platoon Sgt = B

Fire teams

A section is broken down into two fire teams, Charlie and Delta. This allows a section to split into two halves for achieving objectives.

- **Charlie fire team:** Section commander (IC) plus 3 riflemen.
- **Delta fire team:** Section second in command (2IC) plus 3 riflemen.

Battle buddies

Within a fire team of four cadets, there are two pairs. These pairs need to work together throughout any exercise. It is good to stick together for setting up shelter, cooking and eating, checking kit together and patrolling. This builds a bond and means that a cadet is never alone, with someone always watching their back.

Patrolling

A patrol is a tactical walk in a section to achieve one of three main objectives.

1. Reconnaissance patrol: Sent out to observe an area or enemy position.

2. Fighting patrol: Sent out to engage with the enemy.

3. Standing patrol: Sent out to check or maintain security of an area.

At two and three star level, there is a lot more to learn about patrolling including formations and tactical procedures, but for now, this gives you a quick overview.

Field signals

Field (hand) signals play a major part of communication when out in the field, either to avoid speaking or shouting when attempting to remain undetected, or when it is too noisy to shout over the volume of a fire fight.

Basic movement signals

These signals give basic commands around movement. Some of them require passing on to the next person in the section.

Ready to move
Move hand in circular motion in front of body.

Advance or follow me
Swing arm, rear to front below the shoulder.

Halt
Arm raised level with shoulder. (Point to rest area if resting).

Slow down
Move arm slowly up and down to the side, palm facing down.

Space out
Palm of hand facing weapon, moved away several times.

Go back or turn around
Hand circled at hip height.

Close on me
Hand placed on head with elbow square to the side.

Double
Clenched fist, move up and down between thigh and shoulder height.

Move up
Hand open, arm swung in direction required to move.

Freeze & listen
Hand cupped to ear.

Lie down
Push palm of hand down to ground several times.

As you were
Arm extended down, open hand waved across body.

Specific commands: More specific information or commands.

Enemy seen or suspected
Thumb pointed down.

No enemy seen/all clear
Thumb pointed up.

Obstacle or crossing
Arms crossed in front.

Reconnaissance
Hand held to eye, like using a telescope.

Form ambush
Hold hand over face, then point to location of ambush.

Groups: Indicate specific groups or individuals.

Platoon commander
2 open fingers held on shoulder (Lieutenant stars).

Section commander
2 open fingers held on arm (Corporal stripes).

O Group
Move thumb and fingers together to simulate a mouth talking.

Scout group
Clenched fist with first finger upright.

Gun group
Clenched fist raised to shoulder height.

Enemy contact: Give tactical commands which may be while under fire.

Attack
Chopping hand action in direction of attack.

Give covering fire
Weapon bought into aim.

Fire & movement
One hand making a rolling forward action.

Deploy
Arm waved from side to side then point in correct direction.

Left/right flanking
Left or right sweeping movement.

Formations: Give direction as to what formation a patrol should go to.

Single file
One arm fully extended above the head.

Staggered File
Both arms raised.

Extended line
Arms raised to the side, level with the ground.

Arrowhead
Arms forward or backwards at an angle.

Diamond
Arms above head in a diamond shape.

Elementary obstacle crossing

An obstacle is anything that will slow a patrol down or make it vulnerable. It is important to get the balance right between getting past the obstacle quickly to avoid being targeted, but not so quickly that attention is drawn to the patrol.

Tactical approach

There are various ways to acheive the same results when crossing an obstacle, but the concept is always the same; there must always be at least one person covering while the remainder move. The order in which the section moves across is down to the section IC and should be rehearsed by the section before setting off on a patrol.

1. Halt short of the obstacle.

2. Someone scouts ahead to check all is clear.

3. Someone (or more than one) provides cover for the first members to cross.

4. Remainder then cross the obstacle one by one.

5 The first member(s) across provide cover from the other side.

6 When everyone is across, the Initial members also cross and the patrol resumes.

General guide for crossing obstacles

- **Gates and fences:** If possible go under gates and fences, if not go over but try to keep your body as low as possible.

- **Walls:** Assist each other over walls, again keeping as flat as possible over the top.

- **Ditches, streams, hedges and gaps:** Obstacles that force you into a small area are ideal places for an enemy position to observe. Be cautious and get past quickly.

- **Open ground, roads and junctions:** These may also be covered by enemy fire, and may have several different areas of threat to watch for. Use more of the section to watch and observe different arcs before sending anyone across. Once across, everyone should provide cover and watch ahead as well as behind them.

- **When under fire:** If you are in close contact with an enemy, covering fire is needed while crossing an obstacle.

Selecting a route across country

When moving from one location to another, it is important to choose our route carefully. Having learnt about camouflage, concealment and different types of movement, it is now time to think about what type of ground and cover best suit our purposes.

The ideal scenario is to have an easy route that has good cover from enemy observation and fire, and allows us to observe without being seen. This is not always possible though and we have to make the best of what is available.

Types of ground and cover

All routes available have good and bad points so we need to weigh up what is most important when choosing our route. Here are a few examples:

Dead ground

Enemy cannot see anything in dead ground so it provides good cover. It also means you can't see them though.

Streams & ditches

Provides good cover, but are obvious routes so are quite likely to be watched by enemy.

Hedges & bushes

Can provide good cover from view, but not good cover from enemy fire. Avoid isolated cover though.

Woods

These provide good cover from ground and air, but can be easy to get lost in.

Buildings & walls

Provides good cover from view, and if well made, can provide cover from fire.

Farmland

Certain buildings may provide good cover, but animals are inquisitive and may give away your position.

Introduction to night training

One of the best ways to avoid being seen is to work at night under the cover of darkness. This however is not always easy, and provides its own challenges.

Night vision

Our eyes work differently in the dark and are not as effective as during the day. The eye is made up of cones which are used in daylight, and rods which are used at night, and the full changeover from day to night vision can take over 30 minutes. Unfortunately, going back to day vision can take just a few moments and any exposure to bright light can make that happen. Because of this, it is important to preserve our night vision and avoid bright lights such as torches, flares, car headlights etc. Keep one eye shut whenever exposed to white light.

Red light

Torches that have a red filter do not effect our night vision as much and are harder to spot from a distance, so are ideal to use when you need to see what you are doing a bit clearer.

Red light cannot be used when reading a map though, and instead, you should use a normal white light torch with just a pin prick of light showing. Green light is also good for map reading and is also good at preserving your night vision.

 A torch with a red filter is ideal to preserve night vision.

 A torch with the end taped over and a small hole made is ideal for map reading.

Observation at night

Observing at night is slightly different too as the our eye's night vision rods are weaker than our day vision cones and get tired easily. Here are some tips:

Off centre vision: When looking directly at a small or faint object you may not see it. If you look slightly to one side you will see it more clearly.

Scanning: Scan slowly in separate movements and rest for ten seconds every two minutes. If you suspect something, scan it off centre in a figure of eight.

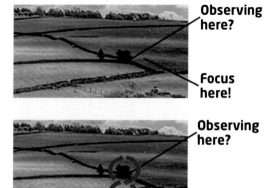

Observing here?

Focus here!

Observing here?

Seeing things

Observing at night can also be confusing, because without seeing things in detail, your brain attempts to make sense of them and can misinterpret what it sees. This can lead to you thinking you see something that isn't actually there, or think an object is moving when in fact it is stationary.

To avoid this, make sure to rest your eyes as often as possible, and don't strain to see things for too long. If an object appears to move, hold your hand at arms length and place a finger in line with it. Having something reliable to compare it with will prove if it is moving or not.

Being seen

There may be occasions where an enemy uses white light to try and see you, this could be in the form of a torch, or in a trip flare (similar to a firework that illuminates a large area). If this happens, it is best to take cover immediately and avoid movement as much as possible.

If your night vision has settled in, immediate exposure to bright light will be disorientating initially, so if there is no obvious cover near to you, just get down into the prone position and keep still. If in woodland, just freeze.

If spotted by the enemy, take cover asap. If not spotted, carefully get away from the light source and take cover.

Sound at night

Sound travels further at night, and when vision is limited, it can be very useful in identifying movement. If you are moving through ground that has loose twigs and leaves etc., be mindful to make as little noise as possible.

If you are observing and looking for potential enemy threats, make sure not to cover your ears (with a hat or scarf), and listen carefully too. If you hear a sound, to help identify what it is and where it is coming from, half open your mouth and turn your head towards the source of the sound.

Elementary night movement

When moving at night, extra care is needed to avoid being seen, avoid being heard, and avoid sustaining an injury. Here are a few other movements that can be used to assist this. They can also be employed during the day if the ground being covered has long grass, dead leaves, twigs or other potentially noisy areas.

1. Ghost walk

This is a more tactical way of walking for when vision is not too impaired by darkness, and you are not silhouetted against a night sky. Keep your knees bent and hold your weight back as you start to step forward. Lift your feet a bit higher to avoid knocking or kicking long grass or fallen branches etc. Gently place one side of your foot down before placing the whole foot and moving your full weight onto it. Use your hands to feel in front of you.

2. Cat walk

This is similar to the Monkey run, but is a lot slower. Also, use the left hand to gently feel the ground in front to remove any twigs or obstacles that could cause a sound if crossed.

3. Kitten crawl

This is a very slow and tiring movement and is only used when absolute stealth and a low profile is needed. Lie flat on your stomach, and use the left hand to gently feel ahead for any twigs or obstacles that would make a sound if disturbed. When clear, lift your whole body onto your toes and forearms, and then lower back down a few inches forward.

Points to note:

• Move silently. Frequently stop, scan and listen.

• If you hear sound, stop and if possible take cover or lie down. Listen for source of sound using the listening technique from the last page.

Stalking

Stalking is moving into an area occupied by an enemy force and observing it without being seen. This brings together most of the elements you have looked at so far including:

- **Why things are seen:** How to remain undetected, and what to look for to avoid possible threats along your approach.

- **Camouflage & concealment:** Making yourself blend in with your surroundings, and staying concealed when moving and when observing.

- **Observation:** Watching the enemy location in a structured way to avoid missing details.

- **Judging distance:** Knowing how far away certain objects or positions are.

- **Range cards:** Making a sketch map/range card of the enemy location (using your skills in observation judging distance).

- **Indication of targets:** If you need to launch an attack, or are compromised, you may need to indicate targets to others.

- **Moving with or without weapons:** Choosing the best forms of movement at each stage of your stalk. Smaller, more stealthy movements the closer you get.

- **Field signals:** If moving in a section, you will need to communicate with signals.

- **Elementary obstacle crossing:** Dealing with obstacles on your route.

- **Selecting a route across country:** Selecting sections of your journey and stalk that best serve your purpose (giving cover and allowing observation).

- **Introduction to night training:** When stalking at night, there are slightly different considerations.

- **Elementary night movement:** More methods of movement to cope with difficult terrain or night time conditions.

Preparation

Before setting off, you need to be aware of a few key points such as the location of the enemy force to be observed, your route in, the best observation locations and where to go to after the stalk. Make sure to change camouflage if the environment around you changes, and ensure you have all you need to hand.

Reaction to fire control orders

In a previous lesson, we learnt how to indicate a target to others by giving a range and indication (location). A fire control order gives this same information, but also tells a particular group or individual to fire on that location in a certain manner.

Sequence of fire control orders

To help remember the sequence of information, we use the word **GRIT:**

G: Group: The group or individual required to fire:

- Section - Everyone is to fire.
- Fire team - Charlie or Delta fire team to fire only.
- Individual - One or two individual rifleman to fire only.

R: Range: The distance away from the target:

- This is given in metres.

I: Indication: Location of target (where to look).

- Reference method - Using points of reference known to the section.
- Direct method - Using arcs of fire (left of arc, slightly right of arc etc.).
- Clock ray method - Using a clock face to indicate direction from a reference point.

T: Type of fire: Speed that you will be firing (covered fully during SAA lessons):

- Deliberate fire - A slow rate of fire, around 10 rounds per minute.
- Watch and shoot - Called 'snap shooting', fire only when you see a target.
- Rapid fire - Faster firing, but still aimed. Up to around 30 shots per minute.

Type of fire control orders

There are four basic types of fire control order:

1. Full: Given when there is enough time to give all information.
Example: "Charlie fire team - 200 - Copse - Left corner - Deliberate fire".

2. Brief: When there is not as much time, but the target is obvious.
Example: "Section - Quarter right - Rapid fire".

3. Individual: When the commander passes on the responsibility of when to open fire to the individuals concerned.
Example: "Delta fire team - 300 - centre of arc - enemy in that area - watch and shoot".

4. **Delayed**: Given early to prepare group for firing, but with a delay.
Example: "Section - 100 - Farm building - Rapid - Await my order" then "Fire".

CHAPTER FOUR

Aim

By the end of this chapter, you will have received the following lessons:

1. Map symbols & catching features

2. Four figure grid references

3. Six figure grid references

4. Estimating distance

Instructors reference:

- ACF Training manual
- ISPEC numbers 4 - 7
- NNAS Navigation handbook

General map symbols; Using collecting and catching features to aid navigation

During your basic navigation lessons, you briefly looked at map symbols, which are small pictures or letters that represent various features on a map. These symbols are normally quite easy to recognise and avoid using lots of text.

Map symbols

Map symbols vary for different types and scales of maps, so it is important to check the key within the marginal information of any map you use to make sure you understand what they mean. The most common maps you will be using will be 1:25, 000 or 1:50,000 scale ordnance survey maps, or military maps.

Here are some example 1:50,000 scale ordnance survey map symbols:					
Footbridge	Electricity line	Cliffs	Slopes	Orchard	Golf course

Here are some example 1:25,000 scale ordnance survey map symbols:					
Main road	Minor road	Footpath	Coniferous trees	Orchard	Parking
Picnic site	Historic building	Viewpoint	Nature reserve	Information	Campsite
Bus/coach station	Place of worship with tower	Telephone	Footbridge	Historic battle site	Wind turbines

Using map symbols

During your basic training you looked at using map symbols. Here is a quick reminder of what they are, along with a new application:

Handrails: Handrails are linear features that appear on the ground and on a map that can be followed to assist navigation.

Collecting features: Collecting features are things we pass and can check off or 'collect' along a route to make sure we are in the correct place.

Catching features: These are features that if seen tell us that we have gone too far, and potentially missed a turning or destination.

Following a route

When following a route on a map, remember the following points:

- Orientate your map to the ground (map matches the ground around it).
- Identify your main handrails to follow.
- Look closely at all the collecting features along your route that you can check off as you pass.
- Look for some catching features that are beyond where you intend to go that will tell you if you've gone too far.

Here is a short route with all of these elements covered. Starting at the campsite (1) and ending at the coach station (6).

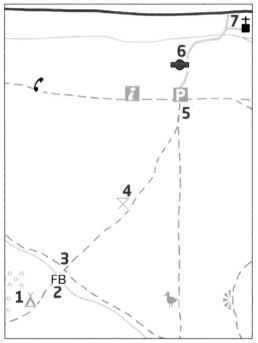

1. Start at the campsite. Orientate your map to the ground, and stand with the orchard on your left hand side.

2. Walk up the footpath (handrail), and cross the river using the footbridge (collecting feature).

3. Go straight ahead at the junction in the footpath (collecting feature).

4. Follow the footpath (handrail), and walk past a picnic site on your left (collecting feature).

5. Walk past a footpath that goes off to the right and enter the car park (collecting features).

6. Leave the car park and walk a short distance along a minor road until you see the coach stop on your left (destination).

7. If you cross another river, and end up at a main road or a place of worship with a tower, you have gone too far and have passed you destination (catching features). You need to go back slightly.

Note: It is important to keep your map orientated and maintain your position by placing your thumb on your last known position. Keep looking around you to identify features that will help to confirm your position.

Estimating distance using grid squares, and four figure grid references

Most maps that you will use have very faint lines on them which break the map into small squares, these are called grid squares and can be extremely helpful.

Estimating distance

Grid squares on maps represent 1km square on the ground, meaning that if you walked a straight line between two locations that were one grid square apart on a map, you would have walked 1km.

Walking diagonally from corner to corner of a grid square is approximately 1.5km.

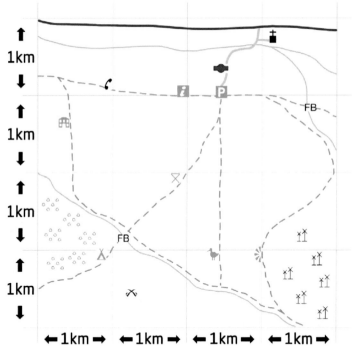

Using this map of a country park, check the following approximate distances. Remember that the paths are not always straight so they will not be completely accurate, but will give you a good idea of how far apart each location is:

- Telephone to information point = 1km (1 x grid square).

- Information point to Car park = 500 metres (half of a grid square).

- Car park to bus/coach station = 250 metres (quarter of a grid square).

- Car park to nature reserve = 2km (2 grid squares).

- Campsite to bus/coach station = 3km (over 2 - 3 grid squares).

Four figure grid references

All grid squares are numbered, making it easier to find specific locations.

The image below shows a small section of a full map with numbers along the bottom (called eastings), and up the side (called northings). The numbers are in line with the grid lines, and cover the square to the right of it (eastings), or above it (northings). To find which square something is in, we work out how many squares along it is, and then how many squares up it is. (Along and then up).

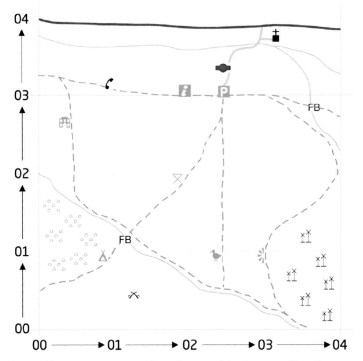

To identify a grid square, we use a four figure grid reference. The first two numbers are the eastings (along), and the next two numbers are the northings (up).

On the map above, the bottom left square that has the campsite in it has the four figure grid reference 00-00. Here are some more examples:

- **Historic battle site:** Eastings = 01. Northings = 00. **4FGR = 01-00** (01 along, 00 up).
- **Bus/coach station:** Eastings = 02. Northings = 03. **4FGR = 02-03** (02 along, 03 up)
- **Telephone:** Eastings = 00. Northings = 03. **4FGR = 00-03** (00 along, 03 up).

  Note: The actual size of the printed squares on your map depends on the scale:
- On a 1:50,000 scale map, the printed grid squares are 2cm x 2cm.
- On a 1:25,000 scale map, the printed grid squares are 4cm x 4cm.

Using six figure grid references

Four figure grid references are great for finding a general area on a map, but because one grid square is 1km square it is not so good at pinpointing more specific locations. For this we need to use six figure grid references.

The map from the previous page has now been zoomed in to show just four main grid squares.

There is also now another grid of ten squares by ten squares which are all numbered in between the main grid square numbers.

These lines and numbers are not printed on maps, so you need to use a romer or compass. These have the lines and numbers printed on clear plastic that can lay on your map.

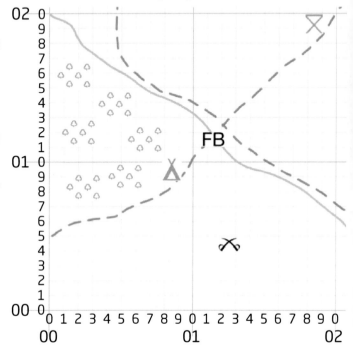

To work out a six figure grid reference and pinpoint a location more accurately, we simply add one number to the eastings, to say exactly how far along the location is, and then add one number to the northings to say exactly how far up the location is.

Example: The four figure grid reference for the historic battle site is 01-00. To find the six figure grid reference, we need to add the extra numbers in.

- The main easting number is **01** and the small grid number is **2**. This becomes **012**.

- The main northing number is **00** and the small grid number is **4**. This becomes **004**.

- The six figure grid reference is therefore **012-004**.

  Here are some other examples:

- **Campsite:** Four figure grid ref: **00-00**.
       Six figure grid reference: **008-009**.

- **Footbridge:** Four figure grid reference: **01-01**.
       Six figure grid reference: **011-011**.

Estimating distance on the ground

Being able to estimate distance when navigating is an important skill to learn. It can really help when finding locations in poor light, or when finding a specific track or path when there are several in the same general area.

1. Estimate distance using the eye

This is covered during your one star fieldcraft lessons. See pages 29 & 30.

2. Estimate distance using pacing

If we work out how many paces we take when walking 100 metres, we can use that to judge how far we have walked. Do the following to work out your pacing:

- Measure out 100 metres using a long tape measure and mark the start and end.

- Walk naturally from start to end (100m).

- Step off with your left foot, but just count every time your right foot hits the ground. This is called double pacing. (Say "and" "one" "and" "two" "and" "three" etc.).

- Complete this four times and record how many steps you take each time.

- Add all four totals together and divide by four to get an average. This is your pacing over 100 metres.

- Use a stopwatch to time how long it takes for you to walk 100 metres as well. You will then know how long it takes you to cover that distance too.

When navigating, you can use this to help you walk correct distances. For example, if you are walking between two locations that are half a grid square apart on your map (500 metres) you just count your 100 metre pacing out five times to arrive at the correct location.

Note: Different terrain, weather conditions, hills and weight of equipment carried will all effect your pacing, so make sure to take that into account when navigating.

3. Estimate distance using timing

Having timed how long it takes to walk 100 metres, you can use that to work out timings for different distances. To work out how long it would take to walk 500 metres, multiply your time by five. To work out how long it would take to walk 1km (1000 metres), multiply your time by ten. This method can be used for any distance.

The average walking pace for most people is around 4 - 5km per hour, so those figures can also be used to make good estimates. Here's a timing break down for those two walking speeds. Make a note of them as they will be useful.

	5km	4km	1km	500m	250m	100m
4kmph	75 mins	60 mins	15 mins	7.5 mins	>4 mins	1.5 mins
5kmph	60 mins	48 mins	12 mins	6 mins	3 mins	<1 min

Summary

Here are a couple of journeys using all that you have now learnt.

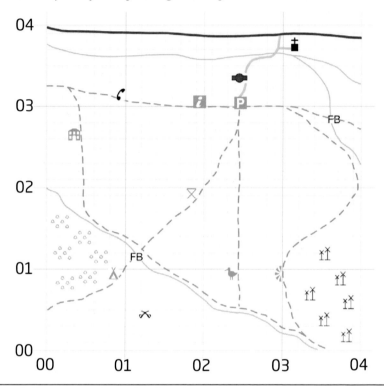

Journey 1: From campsite to bus/coach station.				
Start 6FGR:	**End 6FGR:**	**Distance:**	**Walking speed:**	**Estimated time:**
008 - 009	024 - 033	2.5km	5kmph	30 mins
Handrails: Footpath & minor road.				
Collecting features: Footbridge, track junctions, picnic area & car park.				
Catching features: River, main road & place of worship with a tower.				

Journey 2: From telephone to viewpoint.				
Start 6FGR:	**End 6FGR:**	**Distance:**	**Walking speed:**	**Estimated time:**
009 - 031	029 - 009	5km	5kmph	60 mins
Handrails: Footpath.				
Collecting features: Information point, car park, track junction & wind turbines.				
Catching features: Footpath junction & river.				

CHAPTER FIVE

Aim

By the end of this chapter, you will have received the following lessons:

1. Building the team

2. Expedition equipment

3. Load carrying

4. The campsite

5. Food & cooking

6. Debriefing

Instructors reference:

- Cadet training manual - Chapter 8 - Sections 3 - 8
- APC Expedition training syllabus - Sept 14

Building the team

An expedition is a journey made by an individual or group to achieve a specific goal. For cadets the journey is made on foot, and the journey's goal is normally to cover a set distance or to visit a specific location. Expeditions within the Army Cadet Force are always done as a group, so teamwork is extremely important.

Benefits of teamwork

Being in a team is not always about being with your best friends, so the ability to work with others, be professional and show maturity is one of the most important elements. Here are just a few of the benefits:

- **Effective achievement of tasks:** Working together on tasks such as setting up a tent can be easier than doing things alone, and can save a lot of time.

- **Shared responsibility:** Making decisions in a group means that not just one person is responsible if things don't go right. Everyone then feels like they are part of the process which helps focus the team on common goals and objectives.

- **Pooling of knowledge, skills and experience:** Getting to know each others strengths and weaknesses gives you a broad range of skills to use across the whole group to benefit everyone.

- **Support for less experienced members:** The aim of any expedition should be to complete it as a team, with the stronger, fitter or more experienced members helping those that may struggle more. This creates a real bond within the team, and helps to develop everyone, whatever their level.

- **Tolerance and understanding of others:** Even if you end up on an expedition with your best friends, when tired, cold or stressed, you may end up having disagreements or getting annoyed by others in your group. When working so close together, the ability to tolerate others can make a huge difference. Remember, you may not be acting quite yourself either, so you may require others to be tolerant of you too.

- **Opportunity to trust and be trusted:** Expeditions can have an element of risk or danger attached to them, so the whole team need to trust each other and not do anything that could put anyone in harms way. Being realistic and sensible, and listening to group decisions helps keep everyone level headed.

Expedition equipment

Civilian expedition clothing and equipment can be very different from the military items used in fieldcraft activities. Some items such as wash kit and personal first aid kit etc. (covered in basic training) will be the same, but with items such as clothing and shelter there will be a difference. Here are some suggestions:

Clothing

- **Boots:** Some good quality military boots will be fine for walking long distances in, but some may be too rigid and have poor grip. Make sure whatever you wear, the soles are in good condition and they are comfortable.

- **Socks:** Thick high wool content socks. Wash before first using, and take spares.

- **Underwear:** Ideally moisture wicking, breathable materials. Avoid nylon. Only wear thermal underwear in extremely cold conditions (when moving you will warm up).

- **Outerwear:** Remember to respond to changes in temperature and weather by adding or removing layers. You can wear shorts, light walking trousers or tracksuit bottoms on your legs, and then for your upper body, build up layers from a cotton or moisture wicking t-shirt , fleece or sweater and jacket.

- **Shell clothing:** As a top layer, take a light waterproof jacket and trousers. These will also be windproof, so can be a good extra thermal layer if it gets cold.

- **Extremes:** It is always best to be prepared for sudden changes in weather and temperature especially if walking in hills or mountains, so take a warm hat, gloves and scarf for if it turns cold, and a sun hat and sun cream for if it gets hot.

Personal & emergency equipment

- **Rucksack:** Large enough to take your essentials, but not so big that you pack too much. Approx. 50 litres is adequate. Adjust so that is sits high on your back with the hip pads at the right height. Line with a waterproof bag(s).

- **Sleeping bag:** Same or similar as your military bag. 3 or 4 season and weighing around 2 - 3kg. A 'compression sack/ bag' will help it pack small.

- **First aid kit:** Same as with your military kit.

- **Emergency rations:** Snacks such as cereal or protein bars and hot drink ingredients are good.

- **Wash kit:** Same as with your military kit.

- **Bivvy bag:** Same as with your military kit, a waterproof cover for your sleeping bag that can also be used in emergencies, or to store kit overnight.

Other items

- **Notebook & pen/pencil**
- **Phone/camera**
- **Light shoes or flip flops**
- **Matches or lighter**

- **Eating utensils** (KFS, plates, mugs, water bottle, flask etc.)
- **Cleaning materials** (Small container of washing up liquid plus small scourer or cloth and small tea towel).

Group camping equipment

This is equipment that is normally shared, so load carrying can be split across the team.

- **Tent:** A 2 person lightweight, all in one waterproof tent. This should pack quite small, be easy to erect, and have adequate space for storing wet boots and kit if possible.

- **Stove:** There are various ways of cooking on an expedition, but safety and ease of use are the major factors. Gas cookers with sealed camping gas cannisters are probably the best as they work in all conditions. They are safe and easy to use, and fuel is easy to buy from lots of places. Stoves that use fuels such as methylated spirits are also an option, but are not as ideal and can be expensive. Other options should be avoided.

- **Canteen/cooking sets:** Between the group you will need cooking pots and maybe a frying pan. These are readily available as lightweight nesting sets that pack into one another to save space.

Load carrying

When on any sort of expedition, you will need to take a rucksack of some description to carry all of your equipment. Even if you are not staying out over night, you will still need to take items such as waterproofs, warm top, snacks, first aid kit etc. How much you take and how you pack it will have a big impact on the difficulty of your walk, and how much you enjoy it.

Weight of pack

Although there are certain essential items you must pack, weight must be kept to a minimum. For a guide, make sure your rucksack doesn't weigh more than a quarter of your own body weight.

Here are some suggestions to help keep the weight down:

- **Clothing:** Lightweight, practical clothing. Unfortunately not always the most fashionable, but then not many people will see you, so it doesn't matter!

- **Washing:** Small, travel size toothpastes, soaps etc. are ideal, and you only need a small hand towel. A small pack of baby wipes are also handy.

- **Eating:** Packet foods are lighter and easier to pack than tins, and the rubbish is easier to carry too. Avoid taking luxury items like crisps and cans of drink.

- **Cooking:** Take a small cooker and only enough fuel to last your trip. If using gas, having a small but full cannister is better than a half full large cannister. Take lightweight camping saucepans that stack inside each other.

- **Sleeping:** Pack a lightweight tent that is big enough for your needs but not too big, as this will end up being bulky and heavy. Avoid cheap lightweight sleeping bags that don't offer any real insulation, but try and get a happy medium between insulation, pack size and weight.

- **Other items:** Be sensible with everything else you pack too. Take a small personal first aid kit, not a large pack, and use a small/mini torch or headlight instead of a large hand torch. Avoid taking anything unnecessary.

Packing and carrying

- **Packing:** Make sure everything is packed inside your rucksack (except maybe your ground mat), and try to get heavier items nearer the top. Use waterproof bags to separate items and keep them dry.

- **Carrying:** Carry your rucksack as high on your back as possible, and use the adjustment straps to hold it firmly onto your body without being too tight. If there is a hip belt, make sure this fits properly and sits on your hips to take some of the weight.

The campsite

Whenever possible, it is always best to set up camp at an established campsite, as it will have toilets and washing facilities, and the ground will be suitable for tents. There may be occasions though when you need to set up camp away from a designated campsite so there are a few more things to consider.

Selecting the site:

- Find somewhere that is sheltered from the prevailing wind.

- Choose an area free from obvious dangers such as flooding, animals or falling trees.

- Set up away from habitation, but within easy reach of water.

- Find ground suitable for tent pegs, and reasonably level for a comfortable sleep.

Setting up camp

- Cadets should work together to get tents set up as quickly as possible.

- Set tents up away from any hazards, with the door facing away from the direction of the wind. Tent pegs need to be put in at an angle as deep as they can go.

- All equipment can be stored in the tent, with essential items easy to get to.

Living in the tent

- When sharing a living space so close together, it is important to be organised and tolerant of each other. Respect each others space and work together to keep tidy.

Cooking

- If weather allows, cook away from the door of the tent. If weather is bad then it is possible to stay inside the tent and cook in the doorway but no-one is to leave while cooking, and the cooker must not be under any part of the tent. **DO NOT COOK OR HAVE NAKED FLAMES IN AN ENCLOSED SPACE AS FUMES OR FIRE CAN KILL!**

Hygiene and litter

- This is extremely important, and you can refer to chapter 3 for more details. Remember to wash your hands, face and feet at the end of every day, and wash your hands before preparing food, or after using the toilet.

- All litter including waste food must be placed in an appropriate bin if on a campsite, or taken away with you to dispose of properly later on. Do not bury it.

- When leaving the campsite, make sure to leave it as if no-one had been there. Even if you find litter left by a previous group, dispose of that too.

- In the rare situation where there are no toilet facilities, find somewhere that is at least 30 metres away from water and paths, and 200 metres from any areas such as a campsite where people will be. Human waste needs to be buried in a 6 inch hole, and you need to use biodegradable paper (or it needs to be burned). If you can't dig a hole, spread the waste discreetly and cover with soil and vegetation. Do not squash under large rocks as this will slow down decomposition.

Food & cooking

When choosing food for an expedition, there are a few factors to consider.

- **Weight:** Tins and bulky packs are not suitable as they will add to your overall load.

- **Taste:** You may not be able to have your favourite meal with you, but choose foods that you like and that will give you a boost when you eat them.

- **Easy to prepare:** Items that only require one pot, or that you can boil in the bag are much better than complicated meals that use lots of fuel to cook and leave more washing up. Dehydrated meals are also ideal.

- **Safe:** Fresh foods such as meat and fish are not suitable as you have no way of storing them at the required temperatures, and can lead to illness if not prepared and cooked properly.

Choosing meals

- **Breakfast:** Porridge is ideal as it is small and light to pack when uncooked, and is nutritious and filling. Other items such as protein/cereal bars can be ok, and boil in the bag expedition meals are good although they are heavier and more expensive.

- **Lunch:** Cooking at lunch time is not ideal, so think of some instant options. Crackers or pitta bread etc. with some sort of topping such as cheese spread or meat/fish paste can be good. Cereal/protein bars can also be an additional part. Drink lots.

- **Main meal:** This needs to be a good substantial meal at the end of your day that will replace all that lost energy, and give you a real morale boost. Ideally this needs to be a hot meal, but still wants to be simple to prepare. Make sure to include a dessert.

- **Sundries:** You will also need some snacks and the bits needed to make hot drinks like tea and coffee with whitener (instead of milk) and sugar etc.

Packing the food

When packing, make sure to only take what you need. For instance, if having porridge, measure out enough for the time you're away into a small food bag instead of taking the whole box! Make sure to take cooking instructions if needed and practice cooking new things at home before trying on an expedition.

Cooking the food

- At least one of your meals per day should be hot. Make sure to follow cooking instructions carefully and cook everything thoroughly to avoid illness. Heat meals slowly to ensure they are heated right through and only have your cooker on while cooking. Take a spare bag or two for your rubbish as well.

- After eating, clean everything straight away, and get your kit ready for the next phase of your expedition. If going to bed, leave what you need for the morning out ready. Fill your water bottle and pack away anything you don't need.

Debriefing

Even after many expeditions, you will always learn something new and find ways to improve your experience for the next time. As part of a team it is good to sit down after an expedition, and discuss your experiences together to share this knowledge and learn lessons for next time.

Here are some questions you could ask within your team. Use the gaps below each question to fill in your own personal experiences after your first expedition:

• Overall experience - did you enjoy it?

• Did you achieve the aim of the expedition?

• What did you as an individual contribute to the team?

• What changes to how you packed or what you wore would you make next time?

• What changes to the food you took would you change next time?

• How well did the team work together? Were there any avoidable problems?

• Was there a leader? If so, who? Did it work?

• Did you have enough input into the planning and conduct of the expedition?

• What was your personal high point of the expedition?

• What was your personal low point of the expedition?

• What is the main lesson you have learnt for next time?

• Any other comments or notes for next time:

CHAPTER SIX

Aim

By the end of this chapter, you will have received the following lessons:

1. Overview of the one star skill at arms syllabus

2. L98 A2 Cadet GP overview

3. Ancillaries

4. Marksmanship principle 1

5. Marksmanship principle 2

6. Marksmanship principle 3

7. Marksmanship principle 4

Instructors reference:

- ACF - APC syllabus - Skill at arms and shooting. Version 3: 18 Jan 2016

- AC71807-C (2018): The L98A2 Cadet GP Rifle (5.56mm) and associated equipment

ALL SKILL AT ARMS LESSONS MUST BE TAUGHT BY A QUALIFIED SKILL AT ARMS INSTRUCTOR - THIS CHAPTER PROVIDES REVISION ONLY

Overview of the one star skill at arms syllabus

Skill at Arms (SAA) and shooting at one star level are not completely linked, as you will be learning all about the L98A2 Cadet GP rifle during your SAA lessons, but you will still be firing a .22 rifle (CSBTR) or the air rifle for your shooting test.

During your SAA lessons however, you will also look more in depth at the four marksmanship principles, which will have a direct effect on your shooting.

All SAA lessons for the L98A2 must be taught by a current and competent SAA instructor, and as there is so much material to cover which has to be put across in a specific manner, this handbook only gives you an overview for revision.

Lessons for the L98A2 Cadet GP Rifle taught at one star level

- **Rifle Lesson 1:** General description, safety and the sights.
- **Rifle Lesson 2:** Stripping and assembling.
- **Rifle Lesson 3:** Basic handling drills.
- **Rifle Lesson 4:** Cleaning and maintenance.
- **Rifle Lesson 5:** Holding and aiming in the prone position (1st, 2nd and 3rd marksmanship principle).
- **Rifle Lesson 6:** Firing in the prone position (4th marksmanship principle).
- **Rifle Lesson 7:** Firing drills.
- **Rifle Lesson 8:** NOT COVERED UNTIL TWO STAR TRAINING.
- **Rifle Lesson 9:** Mechanism of the weapon, immediate action and stoppages.

Plus

- The blank firing system.

Skill at Arms Test

- The final test for one star skill at arms is a weapon handling test (WHT) for the L98A2 Cadet GP Rifle. This is not to be completed until all lessons have been received.

  Note: There is a list of elements required for the WHT in the testing chapter, but this is to be used as a revision guide only.

Shooting test

- Full requirements for this are in the testing chapter, but are similar to the basic requirements. You will fire more rounds and be required to be more accurate.

L98 A2 Cadet GP rifle overview

The L98 A2 Cadet GP (General Purpose) Rifle is a single shot, semi-automatic rifle. Unlike the CSBTR which has to be loaded for every shot, this rifle is magazine fed and holds up to 30 rounds. The gas created from firing each round is used within the mechanism to force the working parts to the rear and load the next round from the magazine automatically until the magazine is empty.

Parts of the rifle

Here are all of the main parts of the rifle which you will need to learn.

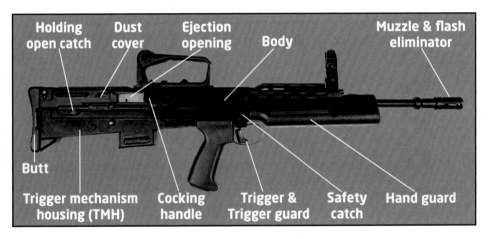

Holding open catch   Dust cover   Ejection opening   Body   Muzzle & flash eliminator

Butt

Trigger mechanism housing (TMH)   Cocking handle   Trigger & Trigger guard   Safety catch   Hand guard

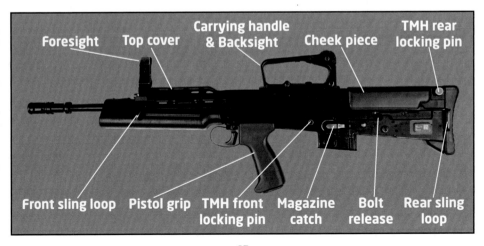

Foresight   Top cover   Carrying handle & Backsight   Cheek piece   TMH rear locking pin

Front sling loop   Pistol grip   TMH front locking pin   Magazine catch   Bolt release   Rear sling loop

L98 A2 Cadet GP: Internal parts

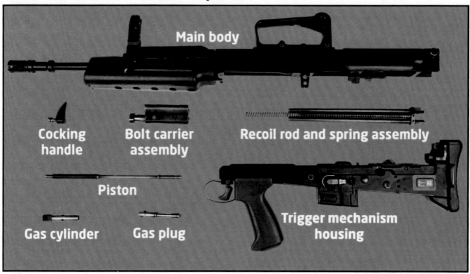

L98 A2 Cadet GP: Cleaning kit

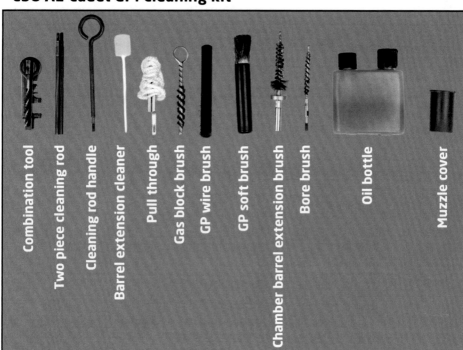

L98 A2 Cadet GP: Combination tool parts

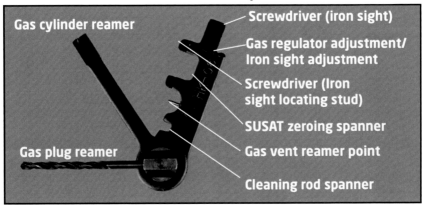

Gas cylinder reamer

Screwdriver (iron sight)

Gas regulator adjustment/
Iron sight adjustment

Screwdriver (Iron
sight locating stud)

SUSAT zeroing spanner

Gas plug reamer

Gas vent reamer point

Cleaning rod spanner

L98 A2 Cadet GP: Ancillaries

Full cleaning kit
Cleaning kit parts are all
stored inside a pouch.

Rifle sling
Attaches via the front
and rear sling loops.

**Blank firing adapter
(BFA)**
Fitted when firing blank
ammunition.

L98 A2 Cadet GP: Ammunition

Drill rounds
For practicing loading
magazines.

Blank rounds
For blank firing exercises.

Ball (live) rounds
For firing on a range only.

Blank magazine
For blank ammunition only.

Live magazine
For live ammunition only.

Marksmanship principles

As a basic training cadet, you learnt an overview of the four marksmanship principles. As your shooting progresses, you can look at these in more depth.

The four marksmanship principles are:
1: The position and hold must be firm enough to support the weapon.
2: The weapon must point naturally at the target without undue physical effort.
3: Sight alignment and the sight picture must be correct.
4: The shot must be released and followed through without undue disturbance to the position.

The prone unsupported position

Leg position 1.
This position ensures that the right side of the body, including the right leg is immediately behind the rifle.

Leg position 2.
This position is slightly angled to the left of the line of fire. The left leg is on the same line as the body, and the right leg is in line with the rifle.

Shooting position checklist

Head low, with cheek resting on the cheek plate.

Left hand under the hand guard, supporting but not gripping.

Butt of the rifle pulled firmly into the shoulder.

Rifle is lifted completely off of the ground.

Right hand is the controlling hand. Hold the pistol grip and pull into the shoulder.

Right elbow in close to support the rifle.

Left elbow as close as possible to a central point below the rifle.

The prone supported position

This position is set up in the same way as the unsupported position except the magazine rests on the ground. This gives much greater support and allows more accurate shooting. Make sure there are no loose stones under the magazine.

Magazine is rested on the ground as a stable platform.

Eye relief

To achieve the best aim, and to avoid the rear sight recoiling back into your eye when firing, the distance between the rear sight and your eye can be adjusted. This is called 'eye relief' and should be set to a minimum of 25mm.

25mm

Aiming

At basic and one star level, your shooting will be done by firing at aiming patches, and working on achieving a good grouping size. Your Point Of Aim (POA) should be the bottom centre or bottom corner of the aiming patch to ensure you are consistent.

When aiming there are four points that need to line up exactly, known as EAST:

E. Eye: Your right eye, looking down the sights.

A. Aperture: The centre of the rear aperture (rear sight).

S. Sights: The tip of the foresight blade.

T. Target: Your exact point of aim on the target in front of you.

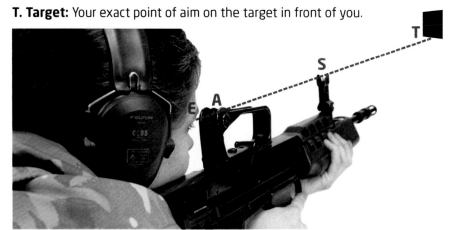

Aim picture

When all four elements of your aim are correct, you will see the following aim picture.

Aperture
(Rear sight)

Aiming patch
on target

Foresight
blade

Point
of aim

To create the correct aim picture, ensure that the tip of the foresight blade is in the centre of the rear aperture, and at the bottom centre of the aiming patch.

Switch your focus between the target and the foresight blade, but focus on the foresight more, especially as you fire.

Testing and adjusting the prone position

After going into the prone position and building up your firing position, it is important to fine tune your alignment and be completely relaxed before firing.

1. Check natural alignment:

• Align the four elements for your aim (EAST) to achieve the correct aim picture.

• Close your eyes for a few seconds and take several deep breaths.

• Open your eyes and see if the aim picture is still correct. If it's not, you will need to adjust your position again to correct it.

2. Finalise position

• Minor changes to your position are done using the lower part of your body.

• To aim slightly left, move your feet and stomach to the right.

• To aim slightly right, move your feet and stomach to the left.

• To aim slightly higher, move your feet and stomach back.

• To aim slightly lower, move your feet and stomach forward.

• Stay relaxed and adjust your position rather than forcing the rifle to line up.

3. Last check

• As you breath in and out, the foresight will rise and drop slightly. Watch this movement to check it passes directly over you point of aim.

Marksmanship principle 4

Having spent time building up a stable firing position, adjusting your body to gain natural alignment with the target, and achieving the correct aim picture, you will be ready to start firing at the target in front of you.

On a range, once you have been given the word of command to start firing ("FIRE" or "GO ON"), you can then release the safety catch (set to 'F' - Fire) and start firing. This stage however requires concentration to make sure the rounds all end up hitting the same area of the target. There are a few more things to consider now to help achieve this.

Trigger operation

First pressure: The L98 A2 Cadet GP Rifle has a two stage trigger, which means that when you first put your finger on the trigger there will be a small amount of slack (no real resistance). After receiving the word of command to start firing, and you have set the safety catch to 'F' (Fire), you can apply a small amount of pressure to take up this slack, and then perfect your aim picture.

Second pressure: When you are happy that your aim picture is correct and you want to take the shot, you can then slowly increase the amount of pressure applied until the shot is fired.

Follow through: It is important that when you fire the shot, all of your movements are slow, relaxed and fluid to avoid any unnecessary movement that may effect your shot. You will also need to hold the trigger in for a second or two after firing before slowly releasing it. Releasing the trigger straight away can cause movement which will effect the round as it leaves the barrel.

Breath control

Breathing is a natural process, so we don't want to do anything unnatural to that process which will have a negative impact on our shooting. We do however want to be aware of our breathing and control the timings of our shots around it.

• Having set up your firing position and received the words of command to start firing, set the safety catch to 'F' (Fire), and take up the first pressure on the trigger.

• Take a few slow deep breaths to increase the amount of oxygen in your blood which will help reduce strain.

• Exhale to the end of a normal breath and then slightly extend the natural pause between exhaling and inhaling.

• Do not empty your lungs completely or hold your breath for too long.

• Apply the second pressure to take the shot when the aim picture is correct.

• If the aim picture is not correct soon enough, it is better to start the breathing cycle again rather than holding your breath.

See the next page for a diagram to help explain this cycle.

Breathing cycle for deliberate firing

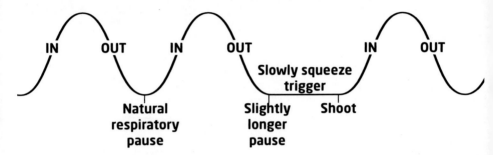

Deliberate trigger operation

The breathing cycle explained on the previous page and illustrated above works for 'Deliberate Fire'. This is when you have lots of time to prepare and take your shot. It is important not to take too much time between shots though as this can be very tiring.

Continuous trigger operation

Faster rates of fire such as 'snap shooting' and 'rapid fire' do not allow so much time to prepare your shots, so you need to apply these principles as best you can with the time available.

Declaration of shot

After firing each shot, look at your aim picture again to see how accurate it is. If it is as you expect, continue on to the next shot. If the aim picture is not correct, or you feel something went wrong somewhere during your firing sequence you can 'declare' this shot to your shooting coach.

After firing a shot, the point of aim in your aim picture is quite likely to be where your round went. This will tell you if it went too high, too low, left or right. You can relay this information to your coach to notify them and they will make a note of it. Simply say "High left", "Low", "Low right" etc.

Declaring shots in this way can help your coach identify areas for improvement in your shooting, and in some cases, during competitions, a declared shot is discounted.

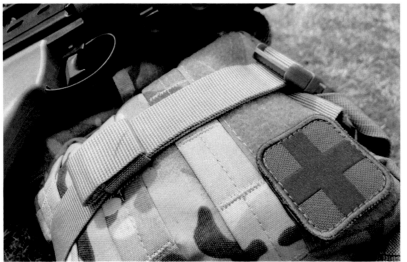

Aim

By the end of this chapter, you will have received the following lessons:

1. Bone, muscle and joint injuries

2. Hypothermia

3. Heat exhaustion

4. Bites & stings

5. Minor bleeding

+ Revision of Basic (Heartstart) first aid training can be completed if needed.

ONLY INSTRUCTORS WHO HOLD AN IN DATE FIRST AID AT WORK OR 18-HOUR ACTIVITY FIRST AID QUALIFICATION CAN DELIVER ONE STAR FIRST AID

ALL TRAINING RESOURCES ARE TO BE TAKEN FROM THE ACFA YOUTH FIRST AID ST. JOHN AMBULANCE TEACH THE DIFFERENCE COURSE. ALL SESSIONS HAVE A LESSON PLAN AND ACCOMPANYING RESOURCE TO ASSIST YOU. EXTRA RESOURCES CAN BE FOUND ONLINE.

Instructors reference:

- First aid syllabus AC71101

- The British Heart Foundation: The Heartstart Course (revision)

- St John ambulance first aid manual (revised 10th edition)

- St John ambulance 'Teach the Difference' Youth First Aid resources

Bone, muscle and joint injuries

Definitions:

- **Fracture** – a crack or break in the bone.
- **Dislocation** – a bone in a joint that has moved out of place.
- **Sprains and strains** – damage to soft tissues.

What you may see:

- Swelling.
- Bruising.
- Difficulty moving the injured limb.
- Fractures may result in deformity/grating bone ends and a wound if the bone has pierced the skin (open fracture).
- Dislocations may result in a shortening, bending or deformity at the injured site.

What you should do for fractures or dislocations:

- Tell casualty not to move.
- Support the injured part if possible.
- Treat for shock if required.
- For open fractures, cover wound and apply pressure around the injury.
- Call 999 or take to hospital.

What you should do for strains or sprains (RICE):

- **R.** Rest the injury.
- **I.** Ice – apply a cold compress or icepack.
- **C.** Comfortable support (apply firm bandage).
- **E.** Elevate the injured limb.

Note: It can be difficult to distinguish between fractures and strains/sprains as they can have similar symptoms. If in any doubt, treat as a fracture.

Hypothermia

Hypothermia occurs when the body's core temperature falls too low (below 35 degrees) for normal bodily functions and can be fatal. It is important to be able to recognise its early stages and take action to reverse it. This topic is particularly important in cadets when training and/or staying out overnight in cold temperatures.

What you may see:

- Shivering.
- Pale, dry skin.
- Feeling very cold and tired.
- If untreated at the above stage, the casualty may become disorientated, lethargic and then unconscious.

What you should do:

- Try to take shelter and protect them from the cold ground.
- Replace wet clothing with dry clothing.
- Give warm drinks and high energy foods.
- After rest and recovery, take quickest and easiest route back to safety.
- If condition worsens, call 999/112 and try to insulate casualty further (blankets/ foil blankets, sleeping bags, body heat).

Keeping safe and warm

Prevention is better than cure. Be sure to anticipate wet and windy conditions. Put on extra layers and waterproofs earlier rather than later. Be prepared to change plans or turn back if conditions become too severe.

Hot food and drink helps keep warm

Add and remove layers as required

Pack extra items just in case

Heat exhaustion

Heat exhaustion is caused by a loss of salt and water from your body through excessive sweating. Be sure to look out for the signs and symptoms below as this can affect many cadets whilst out training. Make sure you drink plenty of water and wear layered clothing.

What you may see as the condition develops:

- Sweating with pale clammy skin.
- Headache, dizziness and confusion.
- Feeling sick.
- Cramps in the arms, legs or abdomen.

What you should do:

- Help the casualty to a cool place.
- Lay the casualty down and raise their legs.
- Give the casualty an isotonic rehydration drink (or water). The ration pack energy drinks are good for this!
- **If condition worsens, call 999/112.**

Staying cool

Prevention is better than cure. Always pack for all weather conditions, remember to keep drinking, and stay covered up when in the sun.

Remember to eat and drink

Keep covered up

Bites & stings

Insect bites and stings are very common, so it is important you know how to deal with them correctly.

What you may see:

• Possible pain, redness or swelling around the site of the bite or sting.

• The severity will depend on what has bitten or stung the casualty.

• A severe allergic reaction is possible.

What you should do:

• Reassure the casualty and scrape off the sting if necessary.

• Raise the bitten or stung part if possible.

• Apply an icepack.

• If the pain or swelling continues, or there is a risk of infection from an animal or human bite - advise the casualty to seek medical help.

Ticks

These are small arachnids commonly found in grassy and wooded areas in southern England and the Scottish highlands. It is important to remove ticks safely using a tick removal tool. An early symptom of lyme disease caused by ticks is a circular rash. Ideally use a tick removal tool and not tweezers to remove.

How to use a tick removal tool.

• Tick removers come in 2 sizes, choose the size that best fits the size of tick.

• Place the fork of the tool as close to the skin as possible under the tick.

• Lift lightly and turn it. The tick removes itself after 2 or 3 rotations.

• If any of the tick remains in the skin, take the casualty to hospital.

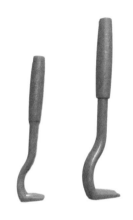

Note: Prevention is better than cure. Wear long sleeved tops and keep skin covered as much as possible when in long grass and woodland.

Minor bleeding

Types of bleed

There are different types of bleeds/wounds:

- Incision / incised wound - clean cut i.e. glass, knife.
- Laceration - tear (sharp rock, barb wire).
- Abrasion / Graze - superficial scratch, skidding.
- Contusion / bruise.
- Puncture wound (nails, bites).
- Stab wound.
- Gunshot wound - entry & exit wound (damage done in-between causes issues).

Treatment for a minor bleed (small graze, cut, scratch)

- Put on disposable gloves, if available.
- Clean by rinsing injury under running water and pat dry.
- If water is unavailable, use an antiseptic wipe (brush away from wound, using a clean wipe each time).
- Clean and dry the area around the wound.
- Cover with an adhesive dressing.

Treatment for a nose bleed

- Sit casualty down, leaning forward.
- Get casualty to pinch the soft part of their nose for 10 minutes and check to see if the bleeding has stopped.
- Try this 3 times for a maximum of 30 minutes.
- Once bleeding has stopped, clean the area.
- If the bleeding does not stop, seek medical help.

CHAPTER EIGHT: Cadet and The Community

Aim

By the end of this chapter, you will have received the following lesson:

1. An introduction to the value of citizenship and service to the community.

2. An overview of the Cadet and the Community syllabus

3. An introduction and overview of the Duke of Edinburgh award) given by the County DofE officer)

4. You and the detachment.

Instructors reference:

- The cadet training manual (volume 1) - Chapter 10
- ac71101 apc(acf)syllabus

Community

The Army Cadet Force is a voluntary organisation sponsored by the Army that takes part in both military and community activities. Its purpose is to develop amongst its members the qualities of good citizenship.

Members of the armed forces have very varied roles, not all of which are of a military nature. Servicemen and women can be seen in the local community taking part in a whole array of different tasks, from attending parades and memorials to helping with major disasters and national events.

This approach extends out to the Army Cadet Force, and you will often see cadets helping in the local community by attending remembrance and armed forces day parades, selling poppies, helping maintain public monuments and attending fetes etc.

It is important that when cadets are seen in public, they display extremely high standards of personal appearance and conduct. In some instances, cadets may be the only military representation at an event and should take extreme pride in wearing the uniform issued to them and show the utmost respect to the men and women that currently serve, have served or lost their lives in the armed forces.

Other services

Other public services that are seen in the local community are that of the emergency services. It is good to know who they are and where they are based.

- Police
- Ambulance service
- Fire and rescue
- Coastguard
- Mountain rescue
- Cave rescue

Discuss these with your instructors and other cadets to find out what services are based near you.

Your detachment

The detachment where you parade is there for you and your fellow cadets to use, so it is important that you look after it as if it were your own property. The staff that are there to instruct you are volunteers, and are not paid to clean up after you. As a cadet you need to take responsibility for the areas you use, and learn how to keep them clean and tidy. Discuss with your staff and senior cadets what it is that you can do to help. Working as a team with everyone doing their bit makes it easy to maintain standards.

Aim

By the end of this chapter, you will have received the following lesson:

1. Revision of physical training in the ACF.

   You will also be required to partake in regular physical training and sports events at your detachment.

Instructors reference:

- APC PT syllabus

Revision of physical training

The physical training exercises for one star are the same as basic training, but when it comes to your test, you are required to do more of them and achieve higher standards.

Warming up and stretching

Before and after any physical training it is important to stretch and warm up. The stretches were all illustrated in the basic handbook, but for revision here is a list:

- Standing hamstring stretch
- Single leg calf stretch
- Standing abductor stretch
- Standing quadriceps stretch
- Bent over back stretch
- Side stretch
- Standing chest stretch

- Standing back stretch
- Tricep stretch
- Lateral shoulder stretch
- Gluteal stretch (knee to chest)
- Seated outside of thigh stretch
- Abdominal stretch

Exercises for testing

For one star testing you now need to complete all seven of the exercises listed, and then use the top six results to get your overall score (scores on page 101). The exercises are all illustrated in the basic handbook, but for revision here is a list:

- Press ups: Hands and feet **OR** Hands and knees
- Trunk curl
- Ball speed bounce
- Bailey bridge
- Single leg squat
- Run (800m)
- Sprint (90m)

Sports and other activities

As well as completing a PT test at detachment, you need to take part in other sporting activities. These will happen on normal parade nights, but you should also look at ways to improve your fitness at home. Activities such as running, walking, swimming and cycling are easy and fun to do, and will help your fitness.

NOTE: Do not attempt any stretches or exercises on your own until you have received proper instruction from an adult instructor.

Aim

By the end of this chapter, you will have passed the following subjects and be ready to move onto two star training:

- Military knowledge
- Drill & turnout
- Fieldcraft & tactics
- Navigation
- Expedition
- Skill at arms
- Shooting
- First aid
- Cadet in the community
- Physical training

Military Knowledge

		Score
Cadet full name		
Detachment		
Company		
Date passed		

Written assessment

A. ACF organisation

1	What is the name of the County/Battalion/Sector you belong to?
Answer:	
2	What does OC stand for?
Answer:	

B. Cadet Progress

1	What rank are you eligible to be promoted to after passing one star?
Answer:	
2	What does JCIC stand for?
Answer:	

Pass: Get satisfactory responses to one question from each section

Assessors name	
Signature	
Pass or Fail	

Drill & turnout

Cadet full name		Score
Detachment		
Company		
Date passed		

Written assessment

		Max. Mark	Pass Mark	Score
1	Briefly explain how to clean your boots			
Answer:		10	5	
2	Briefly explain how to clean your beret			
Answer:		10	5	

Practical assessment

Detail	Criteria	Max. Mark	Pass Mark	Score
1	Attention, stand at ease and stand easy	10	5	
2	Getting on parade	10	5	
3	Open and close order	10	5	
4	Turnings at the halt	10	5	
5	Marching and halting in quick time	10	5	
6	About turn in quick time	10	5	
7	Saluting one the march - eyes left/right	10	5	
8	Dismissing and falling out	10	5	
9	Turnout (ask questions above when inspecting)	10	5	
Totals	(from written and practical assessments)	110	55	

Pass: Score a minimum of 55 points out of a maximum of 110

Assessors name	
Signature	
Pass or Fail	

Fieldcraft & tactics: Part one - Harbour routine

Cadet full name		**Result for all three parts**
Detachment		
Company		
Date passed		

Practical assessment - Overview

There are three parts to the one star fieldcraft assessment, all of which need to be passed to successfully to fully complete a 24 hour assessment. All fieldcraft lessons need to have been delivered, and cadets need to have passed one star SAA to be allowed to carry a rifle and carry out the relevant blank firing elements. Cadets should work in pairs and all carry the correct equipment including rations and 60 rounds of ammunition each.

Practical assessment - Part one (a) - Harbour routine - Sentry duty

One star training cadets have not been taught how to occupy a harbour area so CFAVs are to choose a suitable location and direct cadets into place.

A senior cadet (completed 'intro to leadership in the field') or CFAV is to create a sentry list and monitor its execution.

Item	Criteria	Result P or F
1. Reporting	**Pass:** Reports on time, with correct equipment. **Fail:** Cadet does not report on time or does not have the correct equipment.	
2. Duty	**Pass:** Cadet stays alert and reacts to situations correctly. **Fail:** Cadet does not stay alert or reacts incorrectly to situations.	
3. Handover	**Pass:** Briefs next cadet in detail on the briefing they received and any developments since. (If there isn't a cadet to hand over to, a briefing is given to the section commander). **Fail:** Briefing is incorrect or lacks necessary detail.	
	Total result:	

Practical assessment - Part one (b) - Harbour routine - Inspection

The following is to be checked after spending a night in the field.

Item	Criteria	Result P or F
1. Weapon	**Pass:** Clean and serviceable. **Fail:** Cadet has clearly made little effort.	
2. Boots	**Pass:** Boots polished and in good condition. **Fail:** Cadet has clearly made little effort.	
3. Cooking & eating materials	**Pass:** Clean and fit to use. **Fail:** Cadet has clearly made little effort (appears unhygienic).	
4. Shelter	**Pass:** Clearly provides protection from the elements. Kit packed away if not in use. **Fail:** Cadet has clearly made little effort.	
5. Personal hygiene	**Pass:** Cadet has carried out morning routine and is in good health. **Fail:** Cadet has clearly made little effort.	
	Total result:	

Pass: Eight out of eight correct (parts a and b combined).

Assessors name	
Signature	
Pass or Fail	

Fieldcraft & tactics: Part two - Stalk

Cadet full name	
Detachment	
Company	
Date passed	

Practical assessment - Part two - Stalk

Cadets are to move from a start location to an observation area where they will create a range card without being seen, and then move on to an end location.

The areas should be chosen to allow cadets to demonstrate the relevant skills required without too much difficulty. It should also be obvious where their objectives are.

Ensure there are three easily identifiable objects that can be marked on their range card. There should be at least one CFAV or senior cadet in the observation area to watch for the cadets.

Item	Criteria	Result P or F
1. Camouflage & movement.	**Pass:** Cadet is not observed. OR cadet makes minor mistakes but clearly understands the principles of camouflage & concealment. **Fail:** Cadet is obviously seen.	
2. Range card	**Pass:** Range card is accurate with only minor mistakes. **Fail:** Range card is obviously incorrect.	
	Total result:	

Pass: Two out of two correct

Assessors name	
Signature	
Pass or Fail	

Fieldcraft & tactics: Part three - Defence of a harbour area

Cadet full name	
Detachment	
Company	
Date passed	

Practical assessment - Part three - Defence of a harbour area

The following assessment is done during a simulated attack on a harbour area. The cadets are to react to the command "STAND TO", and then react to two different fire control orders.

The words of command can be given by a CFAV or a four star passed (fieldcraft) cadet.

The enemy can be played by CFAVs or two star passed cadets.

Note: Cadets must be qualified, current and competent on the L98 A2 Cadet GP rifle to take part in this assessment.

Item	Criteria	Result P or F
1. Stand to.	**Pass:** Cadet moves quickly and efficiently into their allocated position and is seen observing their arcs. **Fail:** Cadet does not respond efficiently OR does not move to the correct position.	
2. Reaction to fire control orders.	**Pass:** Cadet is alert, aims in the correct location and uses the correct rate of fire. **Fail:** Cadet does not aim in the correct location or does not use the correct rate of fire.	
	Total result:	

Pass: Two out of two correct

Assessors name	
Signature	
Pass or Fail	

Navigation

Cadet full name		Score
Detachment		
Company		
Date passed		

Practical assessment

Follow a given route covering 2 - 3km depending on terrain. The route should have changes of direction, encourage route following decisions, and have adjacent point features or prominent landforms.

Cadets need to demonstrate to instructors the following skills:

Detail	Criteria	Max. Mark	Pass Mark	Score
1	Using four and six figure grid references.	10	5	
2	Estimate distance by using visualisation, grid squares, distance travelled on the ground, pacing and timing.	10	5	
3	Give a verbal route description of the whole leg to the final destination.	10	5	
4	Maintain position on the map using a combination of handrails, point features and estimating distance travelled.	10	5	
Plus...	Check understanding of basic level skills too.	-	-	-
Totals		40	20	

Assessment date	
Location/route	
Length of route	

Pass: Score a minimum of 20 points out of a maximum of 40

Assessors name	
Signature	
Pass or Fail	

Expedition

Cadet full name		Score
Detachment		
Company		
Date passed		

Practical assessment

Take part in an expedition designed to test the cadets knowledge and practical application of expedition skills. It should cover a route of at least 8km and include setting up a campsite. Ideally the cadets will stay out over night.

Cadets need to have completed one star navigation before testing in this subject. Assessment will be done by observing individuals moving in a team:

Detail	Criteria	Max. Mark	Pass Mark	Score
1	Contribution to the team.	10	5	
2	Knowledge of clothing and equipment.	10	5	
3	Efficient packing and carrying of a rucksack.	10	5	
4	Ability to pitch and strike a tent.	10	5	
5	Preparation of a cooked meal, and cleaning of utensils etc.	10	5	-
6	Participation in the post exercise debrief.	10	5	
7	Post exercise administration.	10	5	
Totals		70	35	

Assessment date	
Location/route	
Length of route	

Pass: Score a minimum of 35 points out of a maximum of 70

Assessors name	
Signature	
Pass or Fail	

Skill at arms

		Score
Cadet full name		
Detachment		
Company		
Date passed		

Practical assessment: Weapon handling test - L98 A2 Cadet GP Rifle

The Skill At Arms test (SAA) for one star is the Weapon Handling Test (WHT) for the L98 A2 cadet GP rifle. This is to be carried out in adequate light by a qualified, competent skill at arms instructor.

As well as for passing one star SAA, the WHT also needs to be completed within six months prior to any live or blank firing. Instructors also need to pass this test within six months prior to any handling of the weapon at all, including training, supervising others and exercises.

NSPs are to be carried out by the instructor on all weapons and drill ammunition prior to any WHT taking place. Tests are to be completed consecutively and are to be carried out using drill ammunition. The ideal ratio is 1:1, but a SAA instructor may assess two cadets at the same time if the cadets cannot see each other.

WHT

Here is a reminder of the procedures that will be tested (using official WHT sheets):

1. Safety

2. Stripping, cleaning and assembly

3. Magazine filling

4. Loading

5. Ready drill

6. Making safe

7. Stoppages / immediate action (IA)

8. IA and loose magazine drill

9. IA and obstruction drill

10. IA and empty magazine drill

11. Unloading

Note: Questions will also be asked during the test.

Pass: Pass in all tests
Fail: Fail in any test (remedial training required before re-test)

Assessors name	
Signature	
Pass or Fail	

Shooting

		Score
Cadet full name		
Detachment		
Company		
Date passed		

Practical assessment - CSBTR or air rifle.

- Two supported five round groupings practice shoot (ten rounds).
- Two supported five round groupings qualification shoot (ten rounds).
- Two unsupported five round groupings qualification shoot (ten rounds).
- Practice shoot scores can be used if better than qualification shoot.

<table>
<tr>
<td>

.22

25 metres

SCORING:

25mm = 25

50mm = 20

75mm = 15

100mm = 10

</td>
<td>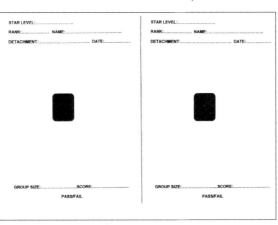</td>
<td>

.177

5.5 metres

SCORING:

13mm = 25

19mm = 20

25mm = 15

32mm = 10

</td>
</tr>
</table>

- Firing at targets similar to those above, fire five rounds at the left hand target and five rounds at the right hand target. Aim at the bottom centre of the black rectangle.

- The practice and first application shoot can be fired supported (left forearm and hand resting on a sandbag (or similar). The second application shoot is to be unsupported.

- Your score is based on the size of your group and NOT closeness to the rectangle.

- The scores from both qualification shoots are added together to get a total score.

Pass: Score a minimum of 60 points out of a maximum of 100

Assessors name	
Signature	
Pass or Fail	

CHAPTER ELEVEN: One star testing

First aid

		Result
Cadet full name		
Detachment		
Company		
Date passed		

FIRST AID MUST BE ASSESSED BY INSTRUCTORS WHO HOLD A MINIMUM OF AN IN DATE FIRST AID AT WORK OR 18-HOUR ACTIVITY FIRST AID QUALIFICATION.

Notes on training and assessments

The assessment is in three parts. These assessments must be taken separately and are "pass" or "refer".

All three assessments need to be passed to fully pass one star first aid.

Full details of the assessments can be found in the First Aid syllabus AC 71101 pages 1:11 to 1:14.

All training resources are to be taken from the ACFA Youth First Aid St. John Ambulance Teach the Difference course. All sessions have a lesson plan and accompanying resource to assist you.

There is no certificate or authorised badge for this course.

The one star first aid syllabus is "Casaid". When Heartstart (Basic) and Casaid have been delivered progressively they match the basic first aid requirement of the Duke of Edinburgh's Award expedition training at Bronze level.

Assessment 1. Pass or Refer	Assessment 2. Pass or refer	Assessment 3. Pass or Refer
Assessed by:	Assessed by:	Assessed by:

96

First aid: Part one

Practical assessment - Dealing with a casualty who is not breathing (CPR)

The cadet is to perform resuscitation alone in a simulated incident, set in a classroom, using a manikin. The cadet is to undertake the test as if the assessor is an untrained bystander to a standard which is effective safe and prompt.

Criteria	Pass or Refer	P/R
1. Assess for danger.	**Pass:** Checks for danger and makes area safe. **Refer:** Does not clear any obvious danger.	
2. Assess the casualty. Response (AVPU), Shout for help, Open airway (head tilt - chin lift) Check breathing (up to 10 seconds)	**Pass:** Checks AVPU, performs head tilt - chin lift effectively and checks for breathing for up to 10 seconds. **Refer:** Does not perform any part of AVPU. Does not open airway correctly and check breathing for up to 10 seconds.	
3. Call for help. Send for AED Gives correct information	**Pass:** Asks bystander to call 999/112 and asks them for an AED. **Refer:** Does not call 999/112 at all throughout whole scenario.	
4. Give effective chest compressions. Correct hand position Correct speed Correct depth 30 compressions	**Pass:** 30 compressions delivered, 5-6cm depth at correct speed. **Refer:** Not able to deliver compressions in accordance with current protocols.	
5. Rescue breaths 2 Effective rescue breaths	**Pass:** Delivery of 2 effective rescue breaths. **Refer:** Inability to deliver effective rescue breaths.	
6. Continue CPR Correct hand position Correct speed Correct depth 30 compressions	**Pass:** 30 compressions delivered, 5-6cm depth at a rate of 100-120 bpm. **Refer:** Not able to deliver compressions in accordance with current protocols.	
7. Questions What would you do if you were alone? What is agonal breathing? What would you do if you could not achieve rescue breaths?	**Pass:** Correct answers to all questions. **Refer:** Unable to answer 2/3 of questions correctly.	
	RESULT:	
	Assessor: Name and signature	

First aid: Part two

Practical assessment - Dealing with a casualty who is breathing but unconscious.

The cadet is to act in a role play incident, set in a classroom, providing care to an acting casualty who has simulated unconsciousness. The cadet is to undertake the test as if they are alone to a standard which is effective safe and prompt.

Criteria	Pass or Refer	P/R
1. Assess for danger.	**Pass:** Checks for danger and makes area safe. **Refer:** Does not clear any obvious danger.	
2. Assess the casualty. Response (AVPU), Shout for help, Open airway (head tilt - chin lift) Check breathing (up to 10 seconds)	**Pass:** Checks AVPU, performs head tilt - chin lift effectively and checks for breathing for up to 10 seconds. **Refer:** Does not perform any part of AVPU. Does not open airway correctly and check breathing for up to 10 seconds.	
3. Carries out quick life-threatening injuries check Removes sharp objects Removes glasses	**Pass:** Does do a life-threatening injuries check. **Refer:** Does not attempt any form of check.	
4. Places casualty in recovery position Ensuring airway is open Body position is stable to allow casualty to be left	**Pass:** Casualty is positioned to maintain an effective airway. **Refer:** No effective airway is maintained.	
5. First Aider goes for help Gives correct information	**Pass:** Calls 999/112. **Refer:** Does not call 999/112 at all throughout whole scenario.	
7. Secondary Survey on return Checks breathing Carries out top-to-toe survey	**Pass:** Checks breathing. **Refer:** Breathing not checked.	
8. Questions What would you do if you suspected a spinal injury	**Pass:** Correct answers to all questions. **Refer:** Unable to answer even after prompting.	
	RESULT:	
	Assessor: Name and signature	

First aid: Part three

Practical assessment - Dealing with a conscious casualty with a bleeding wound

The cadet is to act in a role play incident, set in a classroom, providing care to an acting casualty has cut themselves on a sharp object*. The cadet is to be effective safe and prompt. The assessor is to act as an untrained bystander

* Instructor/assessor is to see specific details of wound in the First aid syllabus AC71101 pages 1:12 - 1:13.

Criteria	Pass or Refer	P/R
1. Assess for danger, and assess the casualty	**Pass:** Checks for danger and makes area safe. **Refer:** Does not clear any obvious danger.	
2. Diagnose Injuries Identify the injury	**Pass:** Locates the injury. **Refer:** Does not locate the injury.	
3. Call for help Send bystander for help Ask them to return with a First Aid Kit	**Pass:** Asks bystander to call 999/112 and asks them for a First Aid kit. **Refer:** No 999/112 call at all throughout whole scenario/does not get First Aid kit at all.	
4. Treatment before equipment becomes available Effective, safe and prompt	**Pass:** Casualty is positioned correctly, and direct pressure is applied. **Refer:** Failure to apply direct pressure.	
5. Treatment after equipment becomes available Effective, safe and prompt	**Pass:** Casualty is positioned correctly, and direct pressure is applied with a suitable, sterile dressing. **Refer:** Failure to apply direct pressure or use a sterile dressing.	
6. Shock and general casualty care	**Pass:** Casualty is treated for shock and candidate is calm, clear and reassuring. **Refer:** Casualty is not treated for shock.	
	RESULT:	
	Assessor: Name and signature	

Cadet and the community

		Score
Cadet full name		
Detachment		
Company		
Date passed		

Practical assessment

Carry out at least three domestic tasks at detachment.

Date	Activity name and location	Time spent	Witnessed by
Total			

Receive the following talks	Date	Witnessed by
An introductory talk on the value of citizenship, a sense of service to the community and an outline of the Cadet and the community syllabus.		
Introductory talk on value of Duke of Edinburgh's Award by the County Duke of Edinburgh's Award officer.		

Pass: Perform a minimum of three domestic tasks at detachment, plus receive the relevant talks.

Assessors name	
Signature	
Pass or Fail	

super
simple quilts
#2

with ALEX ANDERSON
& LIZ ANELOSKI

9 New Pieced Projects from Strips, Squares & Rectangles

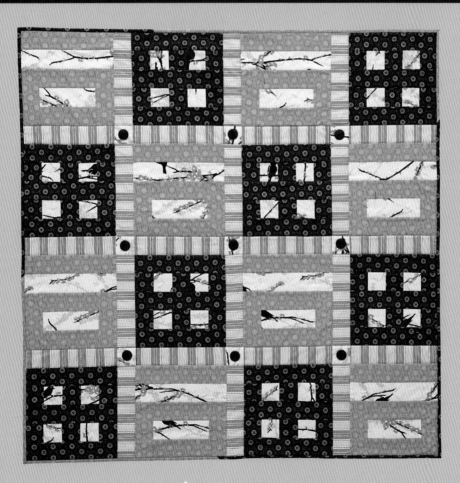

C&T PUBLISHING

Text copyright © 2008 by Alex Anderson and Liz Aneloski

Artwork copyright © 2008 by C&T Publishing, Inc.

Publisher: Amy Marson

Creative Director: Gailen Runge

Acquisitions Editor: Jan Grigsby

Editor: Liz Aneloski

Technical Editors: Sandy Peterson and Rebekah Genz

Copyeditor/Proofreader: Wordfirm Inc.

Design Director/Cover Designer: Christina Jarumay

Book Designer: Kerry Graham

Production Coordinator: Casey Dukes

Illustrator: Tim Manibusan

Photography by Luke Mulks, Diane Pedersen, and Christina Carty-Francis of C&T Publishing unless otherwise noted

Published by C&T Publishing, Inc., P.O. Box 1456, Lafayette, CA 94549

contents

acknowledgments

I'd like to thank Gayle Ronconi for her perfect piecing of many of the quilts, the members of the C&T Publishing editorial department for their ideas and inspiration, and the following companies for providing the wonderful buttons and fabrics used in the quilts:

Dill Buttons

Freespirit Fabrics

Westminster Fabrics

Moda Fabrics

Hoffman California Fabrics

introduction

These quilts can be first quilts for beginners or fast quilts for more experienced quilters looking for the perfect gift, donation, or baby quilt.

This book offers

3 quilt designs in

3 fabric styles in

3 sizes with

3 layer-securing methods and

3 binding techniques.

Choose the size of quilt you want, and from one materials list you can make any of the three quilt designs. This means you can choose a size, shop for fabric (photos of fabric swatches will help you), and then go home and decide which quilt design you want to make. Choose a securing method and binding technique, and you're done! See how easy?

We have included basic guidance to get you started and a great list of books (page 27) you can refer to if you want more information.

I often have the pleasure of brainstorming with Liz. I always treasure the time together. We each bring our own perspective to the table, and more often than not, they are keenly in sync. One such occasion was in the recent past. We were chatting about what sort of book was needed. As usual, life took its twists and turns, and that conversation was left on the back burner, or so I thought. Several months later I received a call from Liz, and she wanted to show me "something." Bingo, her quilts hit the nail on the head. She asked if I would be interested in providing the general quiltmaking instructions for the book and before we knew it, Liz and I were co-authors! We are both very excited about this collaboration— fast, fun, simple projects, perfect for the beginner or the seasoned quilter who wants a quick project, in perfect C&T style.

-Alex

Over the many years that Alex and I have known each other, our relationship has developed through many different experiences: quilt show chairman and vendor, quilting friends/parents, editor and author, and now co-authors. The fun just never ends. With this book, we have combined Alex's expertise in quiltmaking knowledge, with my design and project writing skills. I hope you have fun with the simple designs, techniques, and many options that await you.

-Liz

the basics

 *note* See page 27 for sources of more detailed information.

essential supplies

■ **Sewing machine** (good working condition, with proper tension [refer to the manufacturer's guide for proper adjustment], an even stitch, and a good-quality size 80 needle)

■ 45mm **rotary cutter**

■ 18″ × 24″ self-healing **rotary cutting mat** (must be used with the rotary cutter)

■ 6″ × 12″ **rotary cutting ruler**

■ **Scissors** (small, for cutting threads)

■ **Pins** (thin, fine quilter's or silk pins work best)

■ **Sewing thread** (good-quality matching or neutral-color cotton)

■ **Seam ripper** (sharp, good quality)

■ **Iron**

■ **Safety pins** (1″ long for basting)

■ **Perle cotton or crochet cotton thread** (for tying and big-stitch hand quilting)

DMC perle cotton

Crochet cotton

■ **Needles** (darning or chenille needles with eyes large enough for the perle cotton for tying and big-stitch hand quilting)

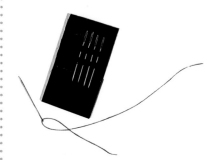

■ **Buttons**

■ **Masking tape** (narrow width to mark quilting lines)

fabric

Use only high-quality 100% cotton fabric. Less-expensive cottons can stretch and distort and be very frustrating to work with.

Always use a combination of light, medium, and dark fabrics in a variety of print sizes. This will result in interesting, exciting quilts.

rotary cutting

■ Practice and learn to use the rotary cutter safely and properly.

■ Cut accurately for best results.

■ Always close the safety latch on the rotary cutter after each cut.

■ Always cut away from your body, at a 90° angle.

■ Hold the rotary cutter as shown, with your index finger extended along the back of the cutter.

Left-handed

Right-handed

■ Place the side of the rotary cutter blade directly against the edge of the ruler.

Place the blade against the edge of the ruler.

1. Fold the fabric selvage (finished edge) to selvage, then fold again.

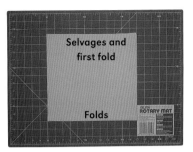

Fold the fabric twice.

2. Align a vertical line of the ruler with the bottom fold of the fabric. Trim to straighten and square up the raw edges.

Left-handed

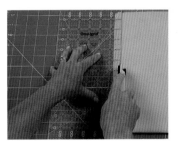

Right-handed

3. Line up the vertical measurement on the ruler with the trimmed edge of the fabric. Cut the size and number of strips indicated in the charts included with the instructions for each project.

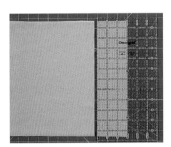

Left-handed

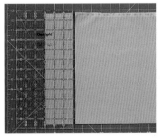

Right-handed

4. Rotate the mat and fabric. Trim off the uneven raw edges to square up the short edges. Line up the measurement on the ruler with the trimmed edge of the fabric. Cut the size and number of units (squares and rectangles) indicated in the charts included with the instructions for each project.

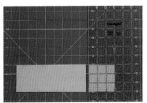

Left-handed

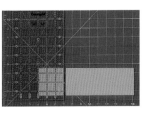

Right-handed

stitching

Straight stitching makes nice straight seamlines.

Use a stitch length just long enough that a seam ripper will slide nicely under the stitches. Backstitching is not necessary because all the seam ends will be enclosed by other seams.

¼″ SEAM ALLOWANCE

Always use ¼″ seam allowances for piecing the quilt tops. This is crucial for accurate results.

1. Raise the sewing machine needle and presser foot and place your rotary ruler under the needle.

2. Lower the presser foot, then manually ease the needle down on top of the ¼″ mark.

3. Place a piece of masking tape along the edge of the ruler to mark ¼″ on the throat plate to use as your seam guide.

¼″

4. Sew a sample to check to be sure you are sewing an exact ¼″ seam allowance.

pinning

Pin at least the beginning and end of each seam. More pins make it easier to align the pieces when you sew.

When aligning seams that are pressed in opposite directions, place a pin on each side of the seam, no more than ⅛″ from the seam.

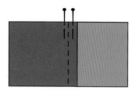

Place pins.

pressing

Press on a firm surface (an ironing board with a single pad).

Press the seams in one direction, not open, as follows:

Place the pieced unit on the ironing surface with the fabric you want the seam pressed toward on top, open the unit, and press. The seam should be pressed toward the correct fabric.

finishing the quilt

BATTING AND BACKING

Batting (low-loft polyester, approximately 2″ larger than the quilt top on each side)

Backing (approximately 2″ larger than the quilt top on each side)

If your quilt top is larger than one width of fabric, you will need to sew pieces of fabric together to make the backing (trim off the selvages first). If you're using leftover fabrics, sew pieces together to achieve the size listed in the Materials chart. You may have enough leftover fabrics from making the project quilts to use for backing and binding.

LAYERING

1. Place the backing wrong side up. Secure the backing to a large, flat surface, pulling the backing smooth and taut (not too tight). Use masking tape to secure on a table or hard floor or T-pins on nonloop carpet.

2. Place the batting on top of the backing and smooth out the wrinkles.

3. Smooth the quilt top onto the batting, right side up.

BASTING

Pin baste evenly across the quilt about every 3″ with safety pins.

note If you plan your tying or quilting design before you pin baste, you can place the safety pins so they will not be in the way.

SECURING THE LAYERS

Securing Method #1: Tying

1. Decide whether you want the knots and tails to be on the front or the back of the quilt.

2. Thread a large-eyed needle with the tying thread. (The quilts in this book were tied with DMC perle cotton or crochet cotton thread.)

note You can use a single or double thread, depending on how much you want the thread to show.

3. Push the needle through all 3 layers, so it comes out through the other side.

note If you want the knots on the front, push the needle in from the front. If you want the knots on the back, push the needle in from the back.

4. Push the needle back through the layers, approximately ⅛″–¼″ from where it originally went through the layers. Pull the thread, leaving a 1½″–2″ tail.

5. Tie the knot as shown below. This knot is more secure than a square knot. Trim the thread ends to the length you want.

A. Tie a half-knot.

B. Pull it tight.

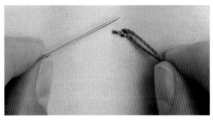

Left-handed

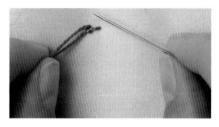

Right-handed

C. Hold the two strands and the needle as shown.

Left-handed

Right-handed

D. Take the needle around the threads. Then, pull the needle through the loops.

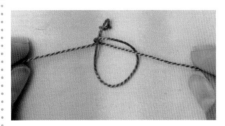

E. Let go of the thread end that is attached to the needle and hold only the short thread tail in your other hand.

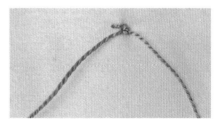

F. Pull the knot tight

 note You can tie on buttons using the same method.

Securing Method #2: Big-Stitch Hand Quilting

note It is not necessary to use a quilting hoop or frame when big-stitch hand quilting, but you have to be very careful not to pull the stitches too tight. You want your quilt to remain very flat and smooth.

The methods shown here for big-stitch hand quilting differ from traditional hand quilting methods because of the thickness of the thread and the size of the stitches.

1. Knot one end of the thread. (The quilts in this book were tied with either DMC perle cotton or crochet cotton thread.)

note Whenever possible, start and end the line of stitching at the edge of the quilt. This will hide the knots. If you have to start or stop the stitches in the middle of the quilt, make your knots as small as possible on the back of the quilt.

2. Insert the needle from the back of the quilt and pull the thread through to the front. Sew a running stitch, making the stitches approximately ¼˝ long.

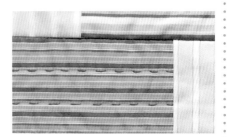

Running stitch

3. When you come to the end of the stitching or have approximately 6˝ of thread left, knot the thread on the back of the quilt as shown below.

Left-handed   Right-handed

A. Take a tiny stitch through just the backing and batting.

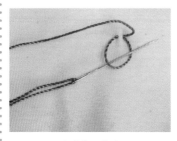 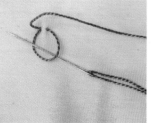 

Left-handed   Right-handed

B. Put the needle through the loop.   C. Pull it tight.

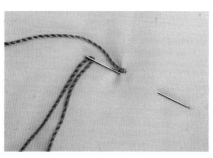 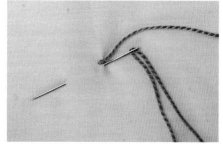

Left-handed   Right-handed

D. Run the needle through the backing and batting about ½˝.

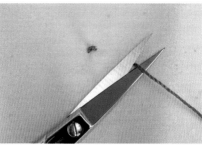 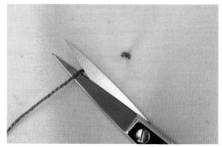

Left-handed   Right-handed

E. Trim off the thread where it exits the batting.

Securing Method #3: Machine Quilting in the Ditch

This is a simple method of machine quilting in the ditch to get you started. Machine quilting takes practice.

note The larger the quilt, the more challenging it is to machine quilt.

▎ You must use a walking/even-feed foot on your sewing machine for the layers to feed through the machine evenly.

▎ Refer to the sewing machine manufacturer's instructions for thread tension guidance. Sew on a test piece of layered fabric, batting, and backing until you achieve the perfect thread tension.

▎ Begin and end the lines of stitching using very tiny stitches.

▎ Use a slightly longer stitch than you use for piecing.

▎ Machine quilt long lines of stitches from one edge of the quilt to the other whenever possible, starting from the center and working out. Then, quilt the shorter lines to finish quilting around the blocks.

▎ Stitch as close to the "ditch" as you can without stitching the adjoining fabric.

Stitch in the ditch.

BINDING

We recommend that you use leftover fabrics for binding and supplement as necessary. You can use 1 to 4 different fabrics. Look at the quilts throughout the book for ideas.

Binding Method #1: Squared Corners, Hand Finished on the Back

1. Trim the batting and backing even with the edges of the quilt top.

2. Cut as many 2¼˝-wide strips as you need to go all the way around the quilt, plus 10˝ or more extra.

3. Sew the strips together using diagonal seams to make 4 lengths at least 2˝ longer than the edges of the quilt.

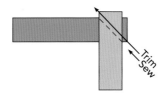

Piece the strips using diagonal seams. Trim.

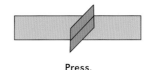

Press.

4. Measure the quilt width through the middle from side to side. Trim 2 binding strips the width of the quilt plus 1˝.

5. Fold the strips in half lengthwise, wrong sides together, and press.

Fold and press.

6. Align the raw edges of the binding along the top edge of the front of the quilt. Let the binding extend ½˝ past the corners of the quilt. Sew using a ¼˝ seam allowance. Repeat for the bottom edge of the quilt.

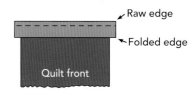

Sew the binding to the top and bottom edges of the quilt.

7. Flip the finished edge of the binding over the raw edge of the quilt and hand slipstitch the binding to the back of the quilt. Trim the ends even with the corners of the quilt.

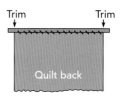

Fold the binding to the back, stitch, and trim.

8. Measure the quilt length through the middle from top to bottom. Trim 2 binding strips the length of the quilt plus 1˝. Fold and press. Align and sew the strips as before, leaving ½˝ of the binding past the corners. Fold over the ends of the binding to create a finished edge before folding the binding to the back of the quilt. Hand slipstitch the binding, including the ends, in place.

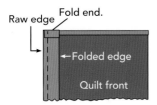

Fold the ends and stitch the side binding.

Binding Method #2: Squared Corners, Machine Finished on the Front

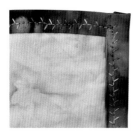

1. Follow Steps 1–5 for Binding Method #1, page 9.

2. Align the raw edges of the binding with the top edge of the back of the quilt. Let the binding extend ½˝ past the corners of the quilt. Sew using a ¼˝ seam allowance. Repeat for the bottom edge of the quilt.

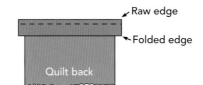

Sew the binding to the top edge of the quilt.

3. Flip the finished edge of the binding over the raw edge of the quilt and machine stitch to the front of the quilt using straight or decorative stitches. Trim the ends even with the edge of the quilt.

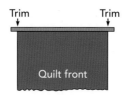

Fold the binding to the front, stitch, and trim.

4. Measure the quilt length through the middle from top to bottom. Trim 2 binding strips the length of the quilt plus 1˝. Fold and press. Align and sew the strips to the back of the quilt as before, leaving ½˝ of binding past the corners. Fold over the ends of the binding to create a finished edge before folding the binding to the front of the quilt. Machine stitch to the front of the quilt, as in Step 3.

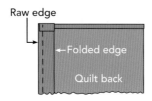

Fold the ends and stitch the side binding.

Binding Method #3: Mitered Corners, Hand Finished on the Back

1. Trim the batting and backing even with the edges of the quilt top.

2. Cut as many 2¼˝-wide strips as you need to go all the way around the quilt, plus 10˝ or more extra.

3. Sew the strips together using diagonal seams to make one long length.

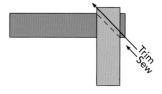

Piece the strips using diagonal seams. Trim.

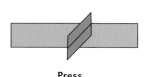

Press.

4. Fold the strips in half lengthwise, wrong sides together, and press.

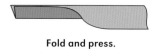

Fold and press.

5. With the raw edges of the quilt and binding aligned, pin the binding to the front of the quilt, beginning a few inches from a corner, leaving the first 6″ of the binding unattached. Start sewing using a ¼″ seam allowance.

6. Stop ¼″ from the first corner of the quilt and backstitch one stitch.

Stitch ¼″ from a corner.

7. Lift the presser foot and needle. Rotate the quilt one-quarter turn. Fold the binding at a right angle so it extends straight above the quilt.

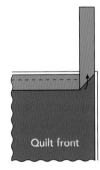

Fold the binding up.

8. Bring the binding down, even with the edge of the quilt. Begin sewing again at the folded edge, stopping ¼″ from the next corner and backstitching one stitch.

Fold down and stitch.

9. Repeat for all the sides of the quilt. Stop sewing 6″ from where you started.

10. Overlap the tails and trim, leaving a 2″ overlap.

11. Turn the beginning tail end under ¼″.

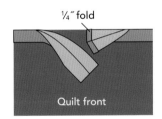

Turn the end under ¼″.

12. Place the ending tail end inside the beginning tail end.

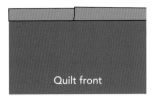

Place the ending tail inside the beginning tail.

13. Adjust to the proper length, pin, and sew to finish the seam.

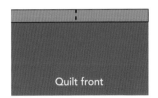

Pin, then sew.

14. Fold to the back of the quilt and hand stitch to finish.

Fold to the back and stitch.

Just So

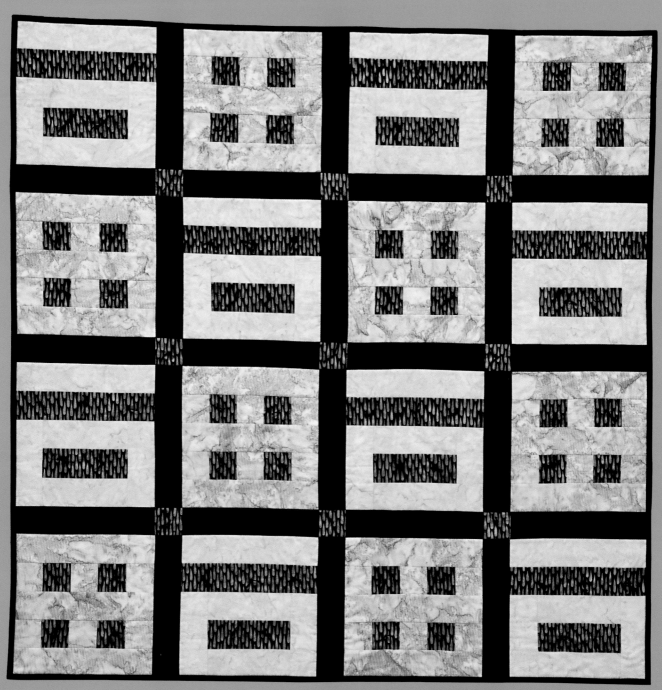

Just So; Batiks pieced by Gayle Ronconi; designed and finished by Liz Aneloski

Wall/Crib: 46½″ × 46½″; 4 blocks × 4 blocks

Twin: 58½″ × 82½″; 5 blocks × 7 blocks

Queen: 70½″ × 82½″; 6 blocks × 7 blocks

Finished block size: 10″ × 10″

materials

Yardages are based on 42″-wide fabric.

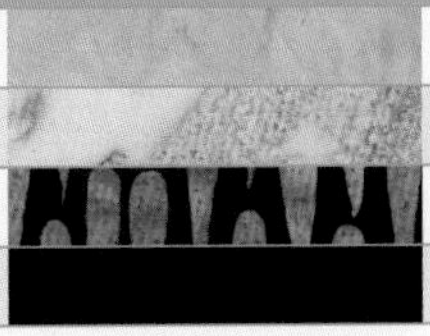

Fabric	Wall/Crib	Twin	Queen
Fabric #1	1 yard	2¼ yards	3⅛ yards
Fabric #2	1 yard	2¼ yards	3 yards
Fabric #3	¾ yard	1½ yards	2¼ yards
Fabric #4	¾ yard	1⅝ yards	2¼ yards
Backing	51″ × 51″	63″ × 87″ (Use leftovers and supplement as necessary.)	75″ × 87″ (Use leftovers and supplement as necessary.)
Binding	½ yard	Leftovers* or ¾ yard	Leftovers* or ¾ yard
Batting	51″ × 51″	63″ × 87″	75″ × 87″

* There will be enough left over to create a multifabric binding.

cutting

Write the fabric name on masking tape and attach to each strip.

Fabric	Wall/Crib		Twin		Queen	
	Size of Strips	Number of Strips	Size of Strips	Number of Strips	Size of Strips	Number of Strips
Fabric #1	2½″ × fabric width	9	2½″ × fabric width	18	2½″ × fabric width	21
Fabric #2	2½″ × fabric width	11	2½″ × fabric width	24	2½″ × fabric width	29
Fabric #3	2½″ × fabric width	8	2½″ × fabric width	15	2½″ × fabric width	19
Fabric #4	2½″ × fabric width	8	2½″ × fabric width	20	2½″ × fabric width	24

making the blocks

Use a ¼″ seam allowance.

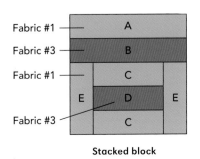

Stacked block

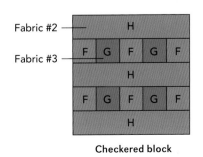

Checkered block

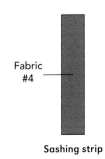

Sashing strip

Sashing square

Stacked Block

1. Place a piece C and a piece D with right sides together. Align and sew along one long edge. Press the seam allowance toward the darker fabric. Repeat to add another piece C to the other side of piece D.

Sew pieces C, D, and C together.

2. Sew a piece E to each side of the C/D/C section. Press the seam allowances toward E. Make the number of Unit 1s specified in the chart below.

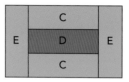

Add E pieces; Unit 1.

3. Place a piece A and a piece B with right sides together. Align and sew along one long edge. Press the seam allowance toward the darker fabric. Make the number of Unit 2s specified in the chart below.

Sew pieces A and B; Unit 2.

4. Sew Unit 1 to Unit 2 with right sides together, matching long edges. Press the seam allowance toward the darker fabric. Make the number of blocks specified in the chart below.

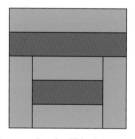

Stacked block

size and number of units

Fabric	Wall/Crib Stacked Blocks: 8 Checkered Blocks: 8			Twin Stacked Blocks: 18 Checkered Blocks: 17			Queen Stacked Blocks: 21 Checkered Blocks: 21		
	Size and Name of Pieces	Number of Pieces	Unit Name; Number of Units	Size and Name of Pieces	Number of Pieces	Unit Name; Number of Units	Size and Name of Pieces	Number of Pieces	Unit Name; Number of Units
Fabric #1	2½" × 6½" (C & E)	32	Unit 1; 8	2½" × 6½" (C & E)	72	Unit 1; 18	2½" × 6½" (C & E)	84	Unit 1; 21
	2½" × 10½" (A)	8	Unit 2; 8	2½" × 10½" (A)	18	Unit 2; 18	2½" × 10½" (A)	21	Unit 2; 21
Fabric #2	2½" × 2½" (F)	48	Unit 3; 16	2½" × 2½" (F)	102	Unit 3; 34	2½" × 2½" (F)	126	Unit 3; 42
	2½" × 10½" (H)	24	Checkered Block	2½" × 10½" (H)	51	Checkered Block	2½" × 10½" (H)	63	Checkered Block
Fabric #3	2½" × 6½" (D)	8	Unit 1; 8	2½" × 6½" (D)	18	Unit 1; 18	2½" × 6½" (D)	21	Unit 1; 21
	2½" × 10½" (B)	8	Unit 2; 8	2½" × 10½" (B)	18	Unit 2; 18	2½" × 10½" (B)	21	Unit 2; 21
	2½" × 2½" (G)	32	Unit 3; 16	2½" × 2½" (G)	68	Unit 3; 34	2½" × 2½" (G)	84	Unit 3; 42
	2½" × 2½"	9	Sashing square	2½" × 2½"	24	Sashing square	2½" × 2½"	30	Sashing square
Fabric #4	2½" × 10½"	24	Sashing strip	2½" × 10½"	58	Sashing strip	2½" × 10½"	71	Sashing strip

Checkered Block

1. Place a piece F and a piece G with right sides together. Align and sew along one edge. Press the seam allowance toward the darker fabric. Repeat to add another piece F to the other side of piece G, then add G, then F. Make the number of Unit 3s specified in the chart on page 14.

Sew pieces F, G, F, G, and F together; Unit 3.

2. Sew a piece H to each side of the F/G/F/G/F section. Press the seam allowances toward H.

Add H pieces.

3. Repeat to add another Unit 3 to another piece H, then add this unit to the section created in Step 2. Press the seam allowances toward H. Make the number of blocks specified in the chart on page 14.

Checkered block

constructing the quilt top

1. Arrange the blocks and sashing pieces. Refer to the quilt construction illustration for the block and sashing placement and number of rows.

2. Sew alternating blocks and sashing strips together to form rows. Press the seam allowances toward the sashing strips.

3. Sew alternating sashing strips and sashing squares together to form rows. Press the seam allowances toward the sashing strips.

4. Arrange the rows.

5. Sew the rows together, pressing the seam allowances toward the sashing rows.

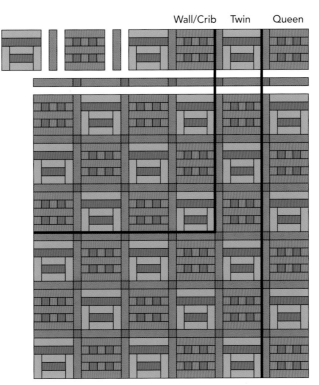

Quilt construction

finishing

Refer to Finishing the Quilt, beginning on page 6.

1. Layer and baste the quilt (page 6).

2. Choose a method to secure the layers (pages 7–9).

3. Choose a binding technique (pages 9–11).

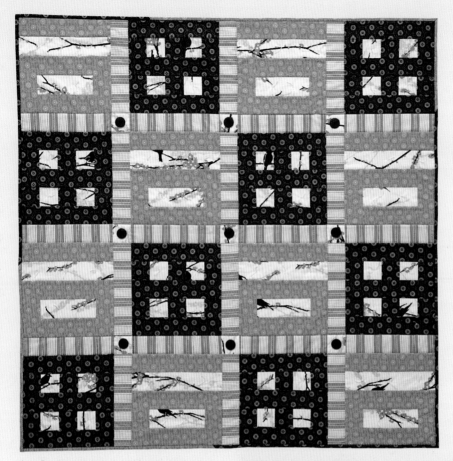

 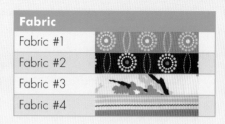
Just So; New Retro pieced by Gayle Ronconi;
designed and finished by Liz Aneloski

 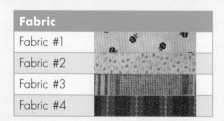
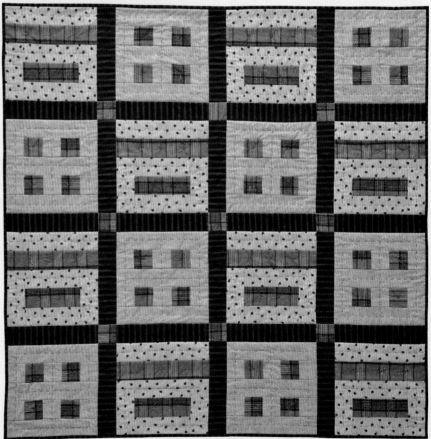

Just So; Plaids/Stripes pieced by Gayle Ronconi; designed and finished by Liz Aneloski

So Woven

So Woven; Batiks by Liz Aneloski

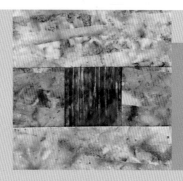

Wall/Crib: $44\frac{1}{2}'' \times 44\frac{1}{2}''$

Twin: $68\frac{1}{2}'' \times 92\frac{1}{2}''$

Queen: $84\frac{1}{2}'' \times 96\frac{1}{2}''$

Finished size: 4″ grid

materials

Yardages are based on 42″-wide fabric.

Fabric	Wall/Crib	Twin	Queen
Fabric #1	1 yard	$2\frac{1}{4}$ yards*	$3\frac{1}{8}$ yards*
Fabric #2	1 yard	$2\frac{1}{4}$ yards*	3 yards*
Fabric #3	$\frac{3}{4}$ yard	$1\frac{1}{2}$ yards	$2\frac{1}{4}$ yards
Fabric #4	$\frac{3}{4}$ yard	$1\frac{5}{8}$ yards	$2\frac{1}{4}$ yards
Backing	49″ × 49″ (Use leftovers and supplement as necessary.)	73″ × 97″ (Use leftovers and supplement as necessary.)	89″ × 101″ (Use leftovers and supplement as necessary.)
Binding	Leftovers** or $\frac{1}{2}$ yard	Leftovers** or $\frac{3}{4}$ yard	Leftovers** or $\frac{3}{4}$ yard
Batting	49″ × 49″	73″ × 97″	89″ × 101″

* Add yardage to match even-stripe fabrics.

** There will be enough left over to create a multifabric binding.

cutting

Write the fabric name on masking tape and attach to each strip.

Place the pieces cut from each strip in a separate stack for easy arranging.

Fabric	Wall/Crib		Twin		Queen	
	Size of Strips	Number of Strips	Size of Strips	Number of Strips	Size of Strips	Number of Strips
Fabric #1	$4\frac{1}{2}''$ × fabric width	6	$4\frac{1}{2}''$ × fabric width*	16	$4\frac{1}{2}''$ × fabric width*	20
Fabric #2	$4\frac{1}{2}''$ × fabric width	5	$4\frac{1}{2}''$ × fabric width*	17	$4\frac{1}{2}''$ × fabric width*	22
Fabric #3	$4\frac{1}{2}''$ × fabric width	3	$4\frac{1}{2}''$ × fabric width	8	$4\frac{1}{2}''$ × fabric width	9
Fabric #4	$4\frac{1}{2}''$ × fabric width	2	$4\frac{1}{2}''$ × fabric width	6	$4\frac{1}{2}''$ × fabric width	8

* For even-stripe fabrics that need the stripes to match horizontally, cut pairs of strips, matching the stripes for each pair used to complete a row.

constructing the quilt top

Fabric #1

Fabric #1

Fabric #2

Fabric #2

Fabric #3

Fabric #4

Use a ¹/₄″ seam allowance.

1. Arrange the pieces. Refer to the quilt construction illustration on page 20 for the block placement and number of rows.

2. Sew alternating Fabric #3 squares and Fabric #1 rectangles to form rows. Press the seam allowances toward the squares.

3. Sew alternating Fabric #2 rectangles and Fabric #4 squares to form rows. Press the seam allowances toward the squares.

4. Arrange the rows.

5. Sew the rows together, pressing the seam allowances toward the Fabric #2 / Fabric #4 rows.

size and number of pieces

Fabric	Wall/Crib		Twin		Queen	
	Size of Pieces	Number of Pieces	Size of Pieces	Number of Pieces	Size of Pieces	Number of Pieces
Fabric #1	4¹/₂″ × 8¹/₂″*	6	4¹/₂″ × 8¹/₂″	0	4¹/₂″ × 8¹/₂″	0
	4¹/₂″ × 12¹/₂″*	12	4¹/₂″ × 12¹/₂″	48	4¹/₂″ × 12¹/₂″	60
Fabric #2	4¹/₂″ × 8¹/₂″*	5	4¹/₂″ × 8¹/₂″	22	4¹/₂″ × 8¹/₂″	24
	4¹/₂″ × 12¹/₂″*	10	4¹/₂″ × 12¹/₂″	33	4¹/₂″ × 12¹/₂″	48
Fabric #3	4¹/₂″ × 4¹/₂″	18	4¹/₂″ × 4¹/₂″	60	4¹/₂″ × 4¹/₂″	72
Fabric #4	4¹/₂″ × 4¹/₂″	15	4¹/₂″ × 4¹/₂″	44	4¹/₂″ × 4¹/₂″	60

* Cut 1 piece 8¹/₂″ and 2 pieces 12¹/₂″ from each strip.

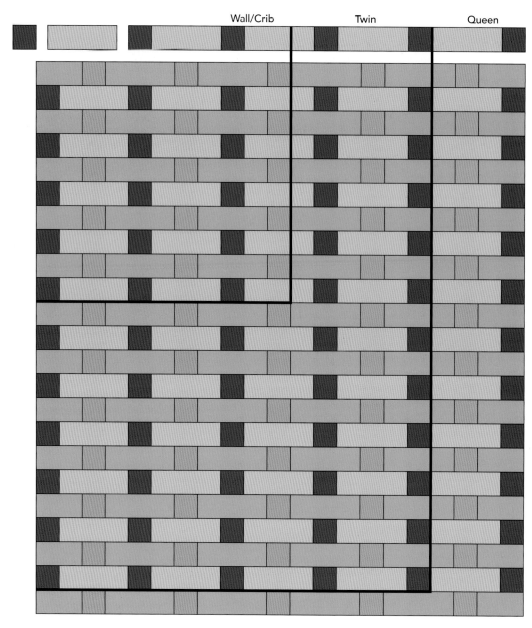

Wall/Crib   Twin   Queen

Quilt construction

finishing

Refer to Finishing the Quilt, beginning on page 6.

1. Layer and baste the quilt (page 6).

2. Choose a method to secure the layers (pages 7–9).

3. Choose a binding technique (pages 9–11).

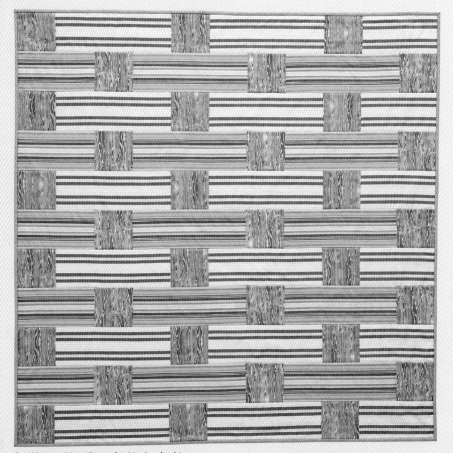

Fabric		
Fabric #1		
Fabric #2		
Fabric #3		
Fabric #4		

So Woven; New Retro by Liz Aneloski

Fabric		
Fabric #1		
Fabric #2		
Fabric #3		
Fabric #4		

So Woven; Plaids/Stripes by Liz Aneloski

So Simple

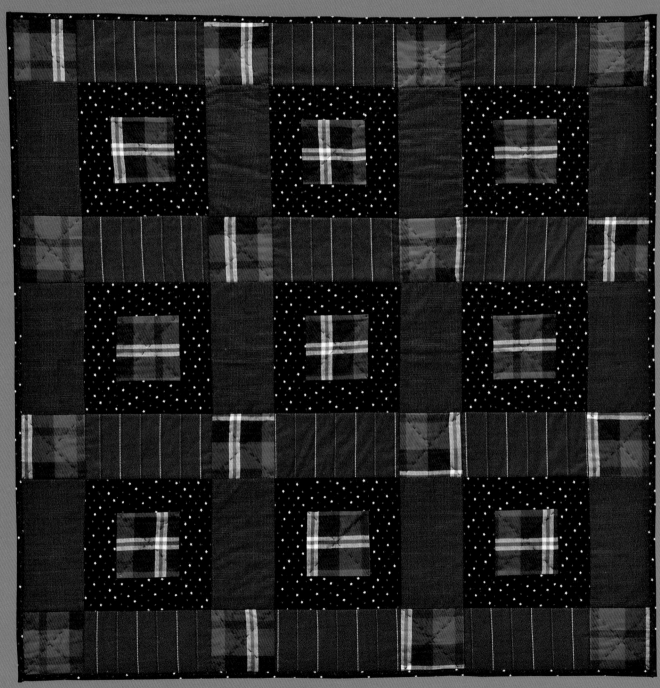

So Simple; Plaids/Stripes by Liz Aneloski

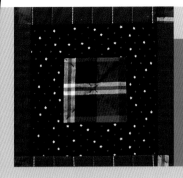

Wall/Crib: 40½″ × 40½″; 3 blocks × 3 blocks

Twin: 64½″ × 88½″; 5 blocks × 7 blocks

Queen: 88½″ × 100½″; 7 blocks × 8 blocks

Finished block size: 8″ × 8″

materials

Yardages are based on 42″-wide fabric.

Fabric	Wall/Crib	Twin	Queen
Fabric #1	1 yard	2¼ yards	3⅛ yards
Fabric #2	1 yard	2¼ yards	3 yards
Fabric #3	¾ yard	1½ yards	2¼ yards
Fabric #4	¾ yard	1⅝ yards	2¼ yards
Backing	45″ × 45″ (Use leftovers and supplement as necessary.)	69″ × 93″ (Use leftovers and supplement as necessary.)	93″ × 105″ (Use leftovers and supplement as necessary.)
Binding	Leftovers* or ½ yard	Leftovers* or ¾ yard	Leftovers* or ¾ yard
Batting	45″ × 45″	69″ × 93″	93″ × 105″

* There will be enough left over to create a multifabric binding.

cutting

Write the fabric name on masking tape and attach to each strip.

Fabric	Wall/Crib Size of Strips	Number of Strips	Twin Size of Strips	Number of Strips	Queen Size of Strips	Number of Strips
Fabric #1	2½″ × fabric width	8	2½″ × fabric width	27	2½″ × fabric width	42
Fabric #2	4½″ × fabric width	3	4½″ × fabric width	11	4½″ × fabric width	16
Fabric #3	4½″ × fabric width	3	4½″ × fabric width	10	4½″ × fabric width	16
Fabric #4	4½″ × fabric width	4	4½″ × fabric width	11	4½″ × fabric width	16

making the blocks

Use a ¼″ seam allowance.

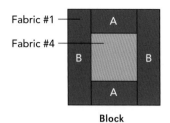

Fabric #1 —
Fabric #4 —

Block

Fabric #2

Vertical sashing

Fabric #3

Horizontal sashing

Fabric #4

Sashing square

Block

1. Place a piece A and a Fabric #4 square with right sides together. Align and sew along one long edge. Press the seam allowance toward the darker fabric. Repeat to add another piece A to the other side of the Fabric #4 square.

Sew A pieces and Fabric #4 square together.

2. Sew a piece B to each side of the A/square/A section. Press the seam allowances toward B. Make the number of blocks specified in the chart below.

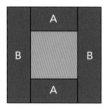

Add B pieces.

size and number of pieces

Fabric	Wall/Crib Blocks: 9		Twin Blocks: 35		Queen Blocks: 56	
	Size and Name of Pieces	Number of Pieces	Size and Name of Pieces	Number of Pieces	Size and Name of Pieces	Number of Pieces
Fabric #1	2½″ × 4½″ (A)	18	2½″ × 4½″ (A)	70	2½″ × 4½″ (A)	112
	2½″ × 8½″ (B)	18	2½″ × 8½″ (B)	70	2½″ × 8½″ (B)	112
Fabric #2	4½″ × 8½″	12	4½″ × 8½″	42	4½″ × 8½″	64
Fabric #3	4½″ × 8½″	12	4½″ × 8½″	40	4½″ × 8½″	63
Fabric #4	4½″ × 4½″	25	4½″ × 4½″	83	4½″ × 4½″	128

constructing the quilt top

1. Arrange the blocks and sashing pieces. Refer to the quilt construction illustration for the block and sashing placement and number of rows.

2. Sew alternating horizontal sashing strips and sashing squares together to form rows. Press the seam allowances toward the sashing strips.

3. Sew alternating blocks and vertical sashing strips together to form rows. Press the seam allowances toward the sashing strips.

4. Arrange the rows.

5. Sew the rows together, pressing the seam allowances toward the horizontal sashing/sashing square rows.

finishing

Refer to Finishing the Quilt, beginning on page 6.

1. Layer and baste the quilt (page 6).

2. Choose a method to secure the layers (pages 7–9).

3. Choose a binding technique (pages 9–11).

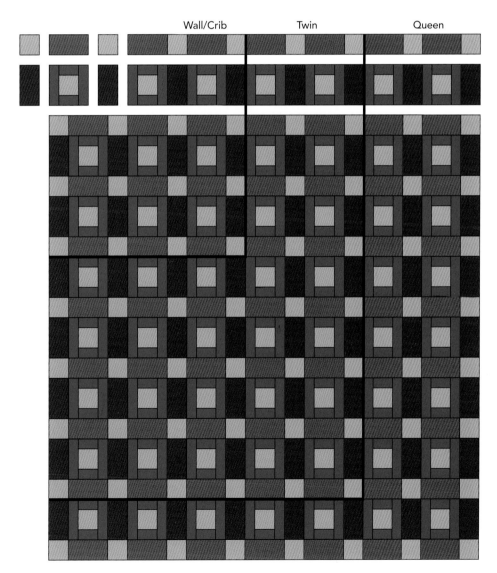

Quilt construction

So Simple; New Retro by Liz Aneloski

Fabric		
Fabric #1		
Fabric #2		
Fabric #3		
Fabric #4		

Fabric		
Fabric #1		
Fabric #2		
Fabric #3		
Fabric #4		

So Simple; Batiks pieced by Gayle Ronconi; designed and finished by Liz Aneloski

resources

For more information, ask for a free catalog:

C&T Publishing
P.O. Box 1456
Lafayette, CA 94549
(800) 284-1114
email: ctinfo@ctpub.com
website: www.ctpub.com

For quilting supplies:

Cotton Patch
1025 Brown Avenue
Lafayette, CA 94549
(800) 835-4418
(925) 283-7883
email: CottonPa@aol.com
website: www.quiltusa.com

other books by Alex:

other books by Liz:

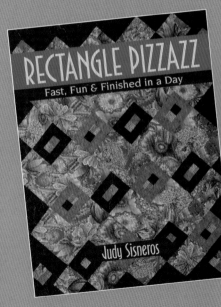
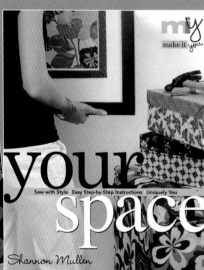